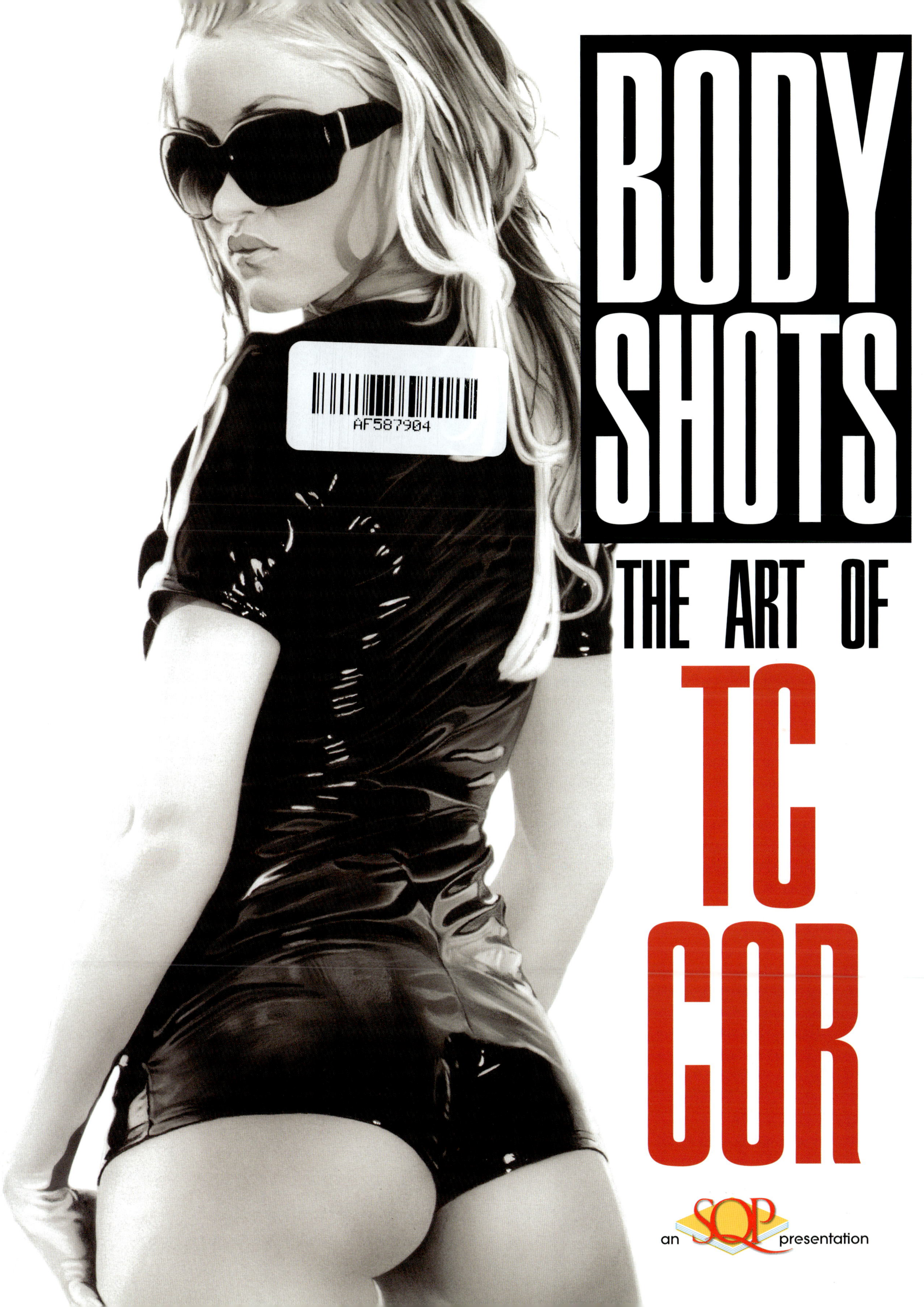
BODY
SHOTS
THE ART OF
TC
COR
an SQP presentation

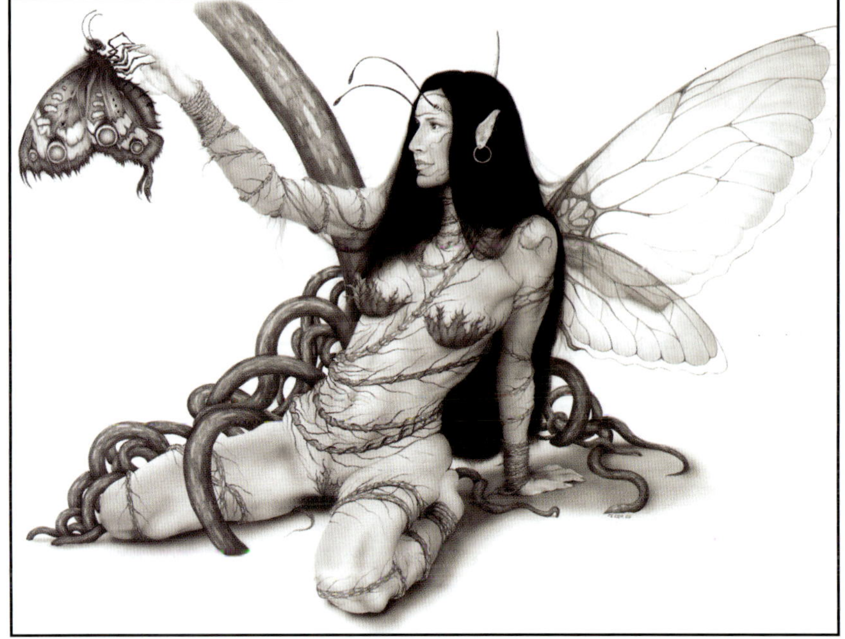

FOREWORD by DAVE NESTLER

Any viable art movement that has enjoyed continued success relies on a couple of important factors. A constant influx of quality work... an increasing visibility in the market, and the initiative to take it's core foundations into new directions. Pinup art is on the cusp of such movement. For the past twenty years, we've seen a sizable shift from the Glamour, and cheese-cake art that proliferated the 50's and 60's, towards a more contemporary version. This new direction not only retains the original artistic values that celebrated the female form of the past, but elevates it to a level that is more representative of our present culture and environment.

There is currently a handful of artists that are leading the charge for contemporary pinup art. And TC Cor is clearly among the front runners immersed in the pack. Armed with a photo-realistic style and an incredible attention to detail... TC has created a body of work that not only defines contemporary Pin-up Art... but flourishes in it.

Dave Nestler
www.davenestler.com

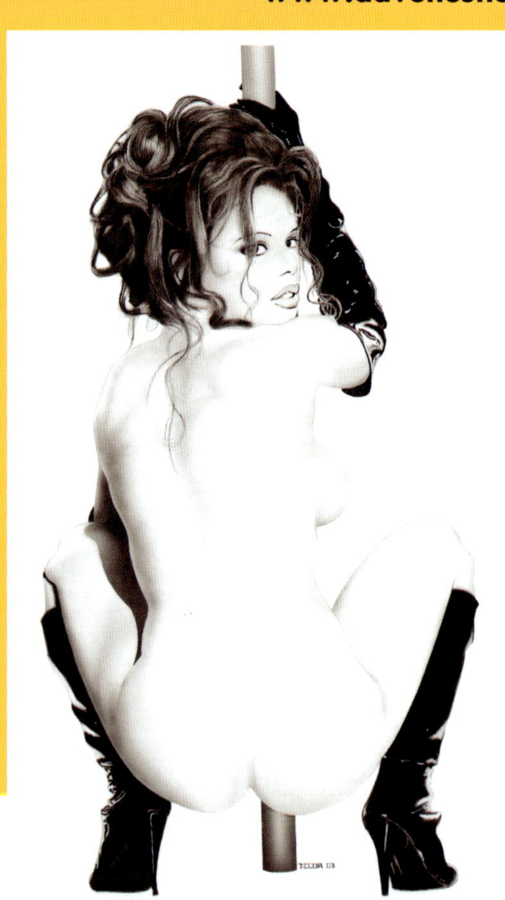

As both a fan and a student of pin-up illustration, it's an honor to keep this uniquely American tradition alive and rolling into the 21st Century. This book contains some of my favorite works of the past few years, focusing on the feminine mystique (with all their delightful curves and angles!). All the works shown are done using traditional methods of drawing with a touch of modern day technical assist. I've used the female form to inspire and improve my level of drawing skills and techniques in both pencil and airbrush. I hope you enjoy them as much as I enjoyed creating them.

To be honest not all the credit should go to me. I would also like to offer some respect and thanks to photographers such as Tim Heffernan, Arturo Jaurequi, and Jefferson Peak to name a few for their professional eye behind the lens. Their work provides me with invaluable photo references that helped make these drawings possible. And of course we can't forget the stars of the show... the models Sivan Krispin, Magen Daniels, and Natalie Lynn and the many others for their beauty and talent which I'm given the opportunity to illustrate.

Most importantly I would like to thank my wife Karen and son Gavin for their support, patience, and understanding with the time I have to spend in the studio behind the drawing board. Finally, a very special thanks to artist Dave Nestler for his support and inspiring words over the years. It's been a genuine comfort to have such a great friend in my corner.

TC Cor
www.tccorillustrations.com

Body Shots - The Art of TC Cor

Book design by Grassy Knoll Studios.

Published by SQP Inc.
PO Box 248 - Columbus NJ 08022

Sal Quartuccio & Bob Keenan - Publishers

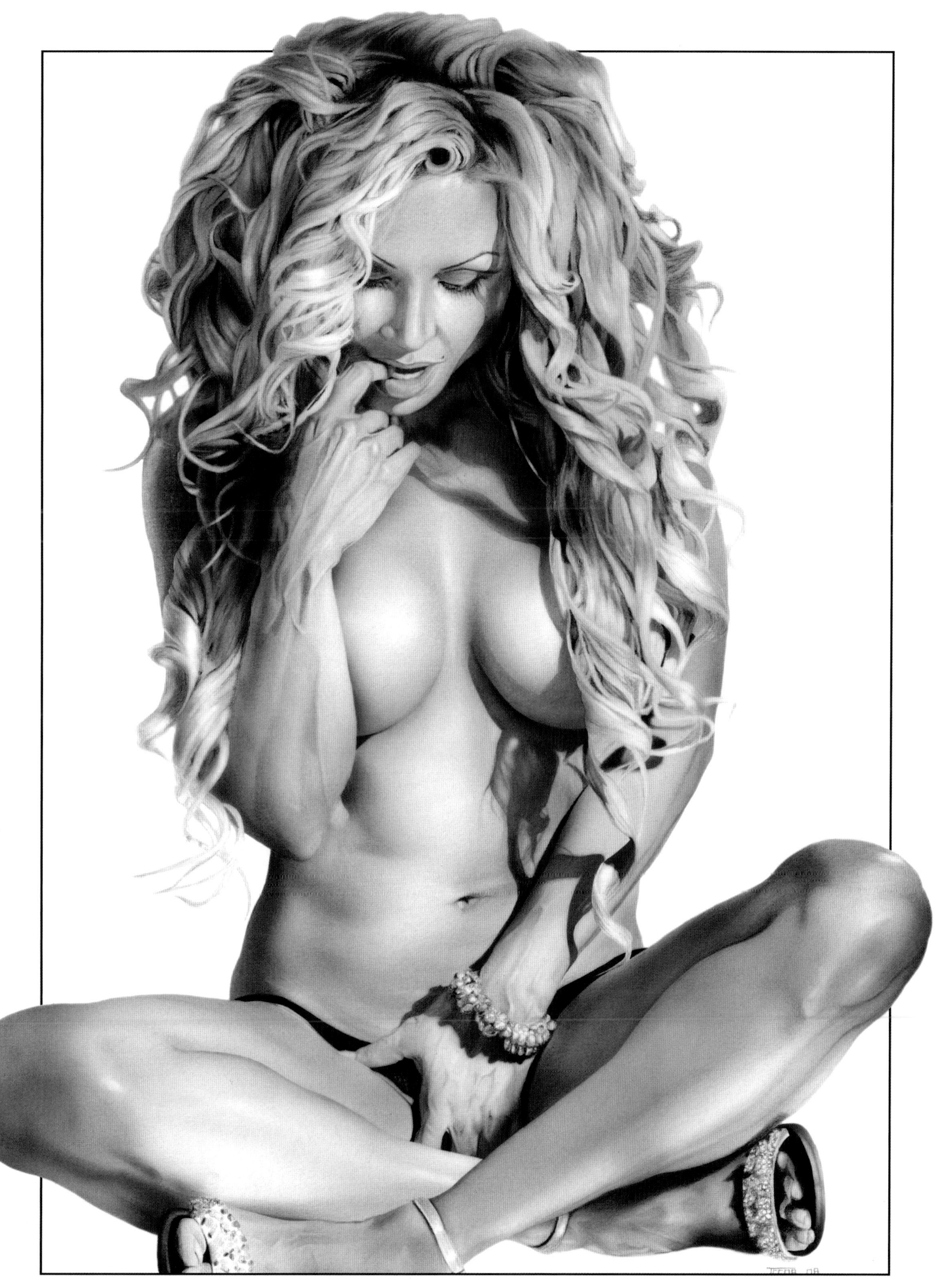

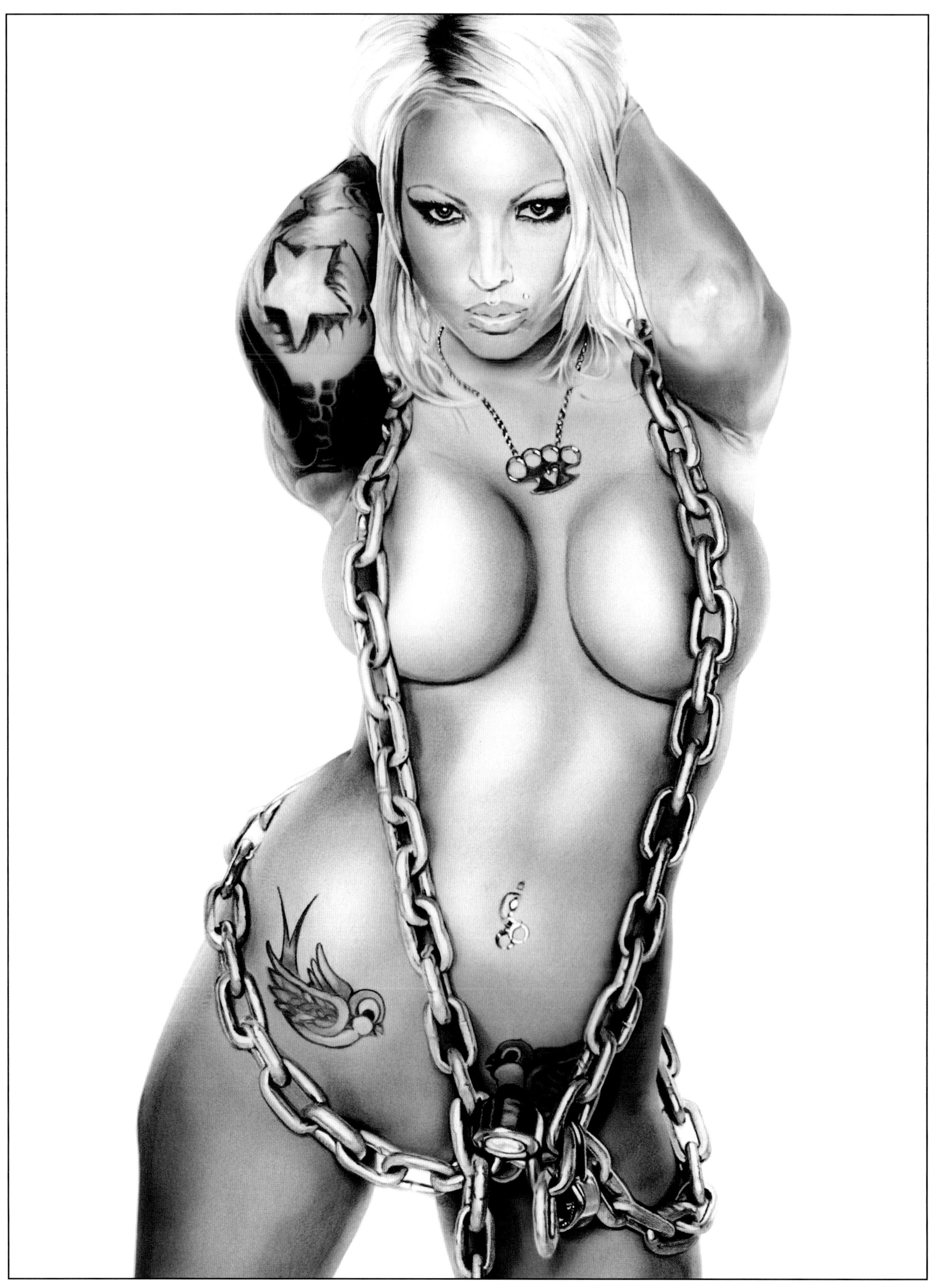

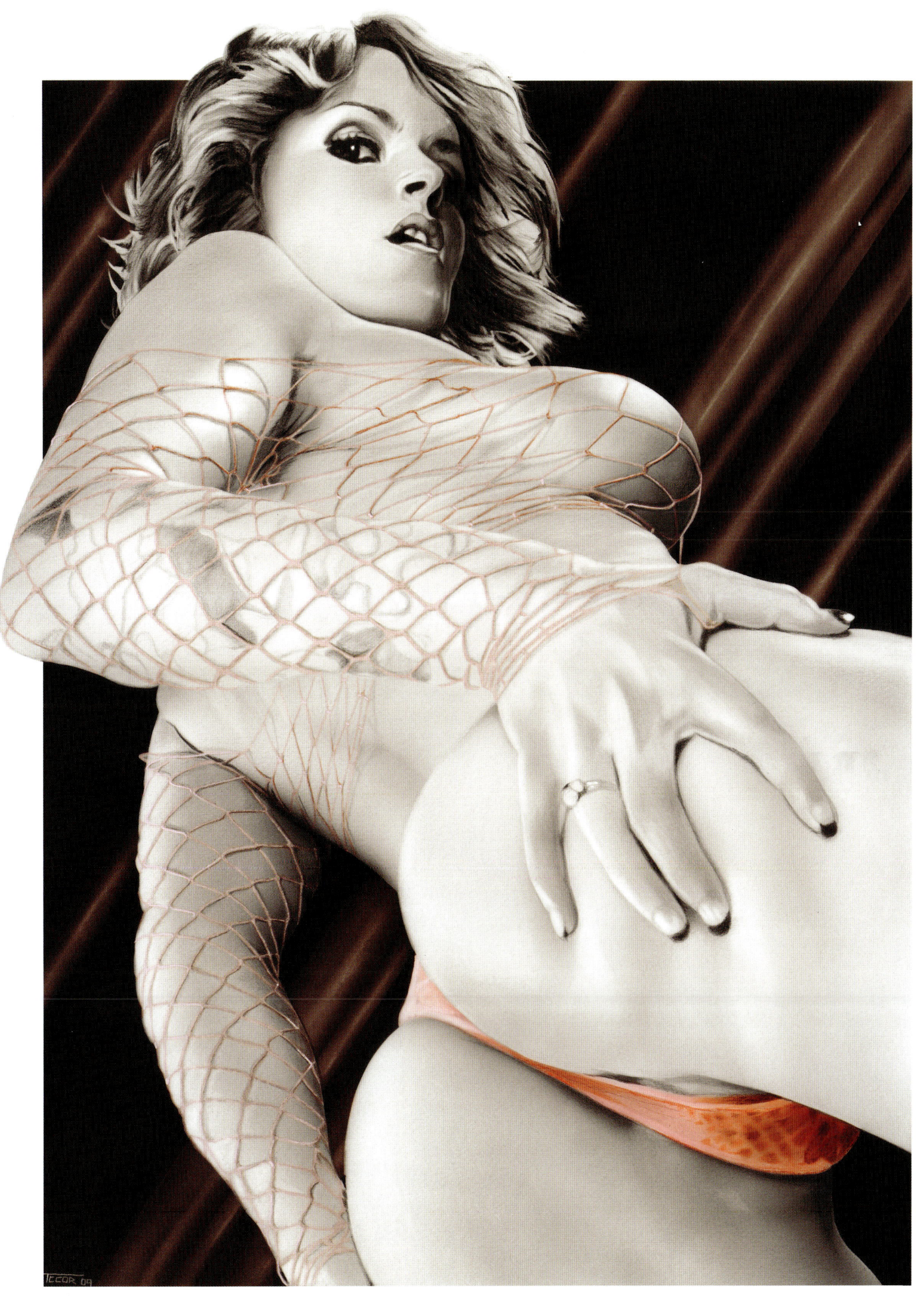
TCCOR 09

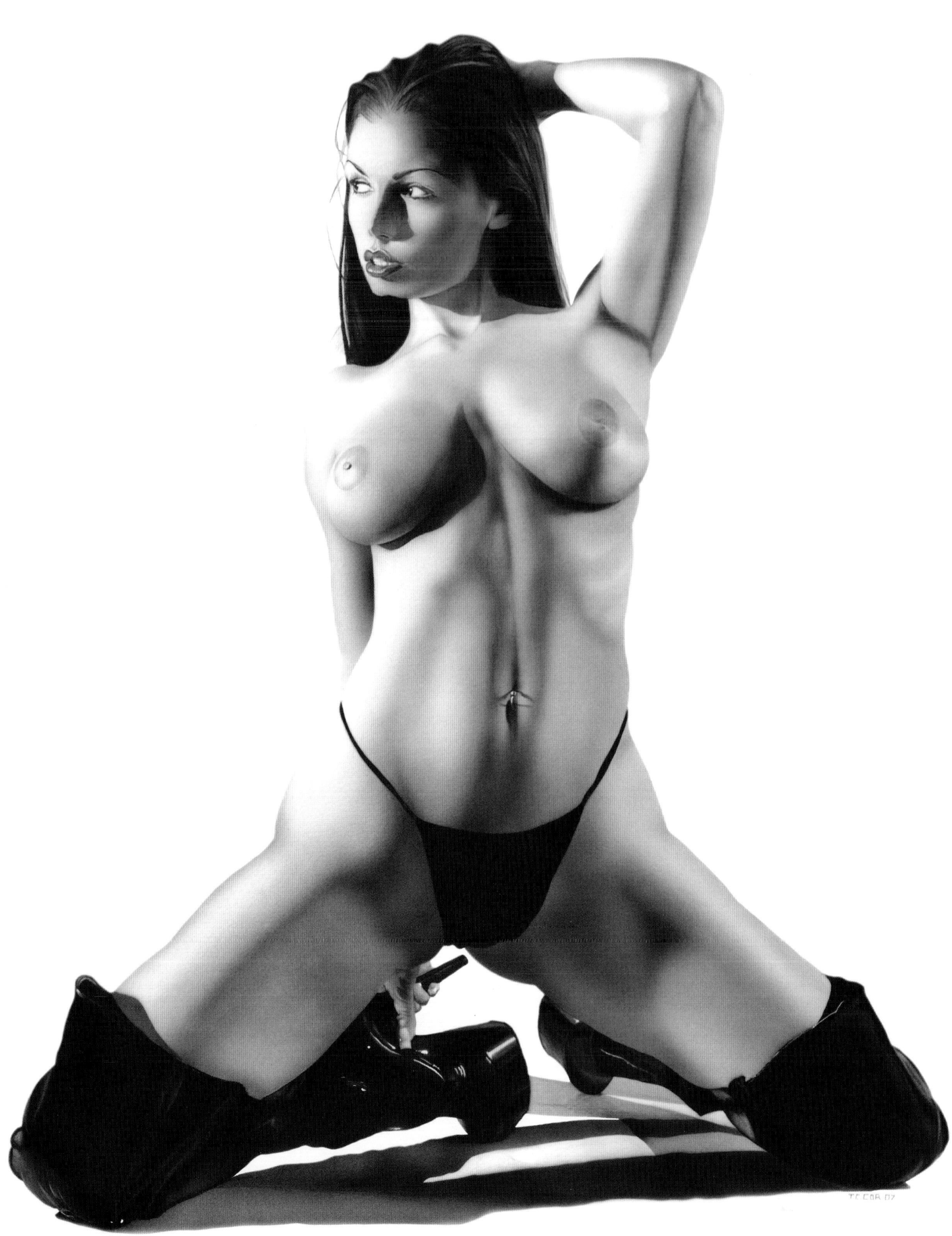
TC COR 07

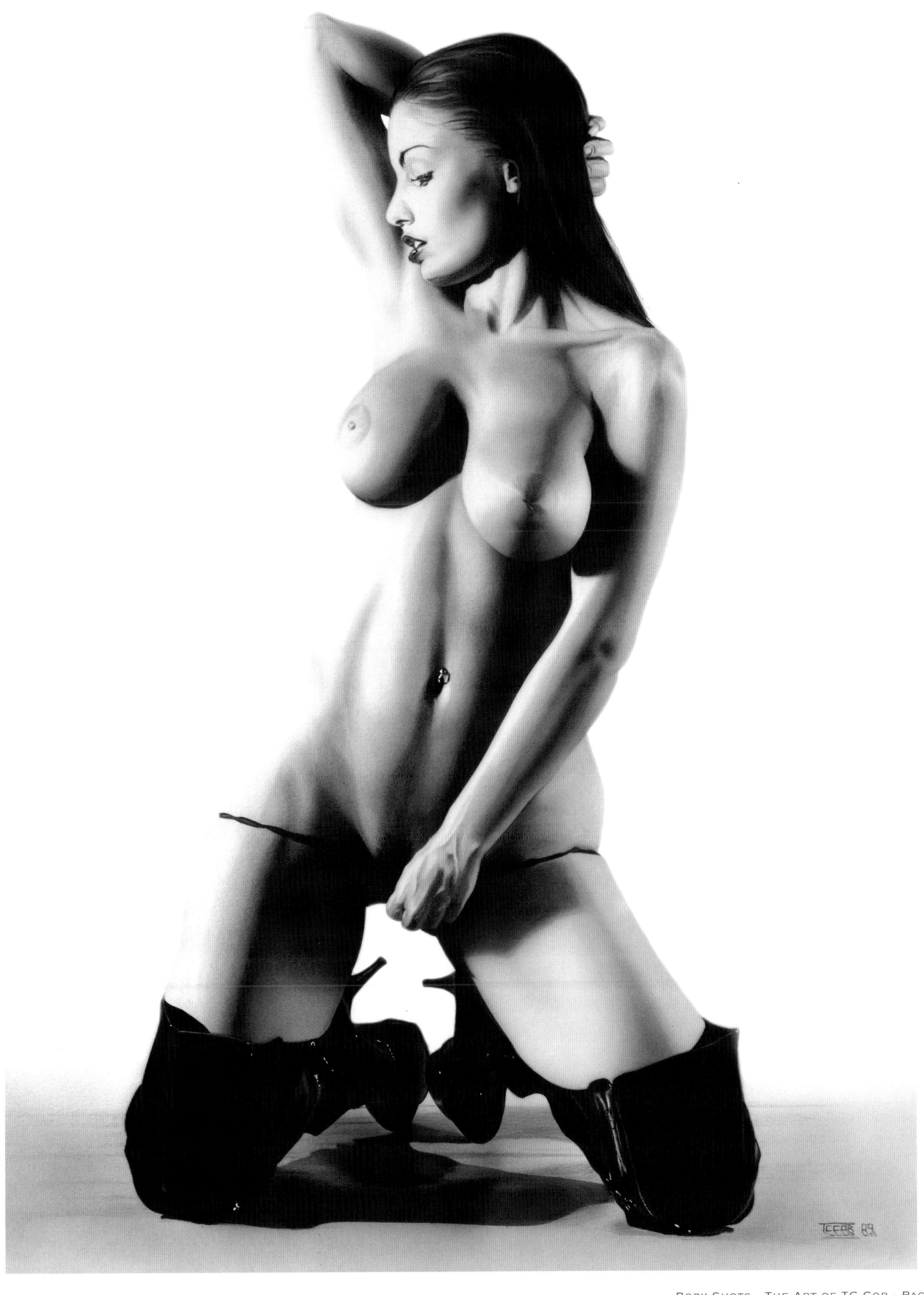

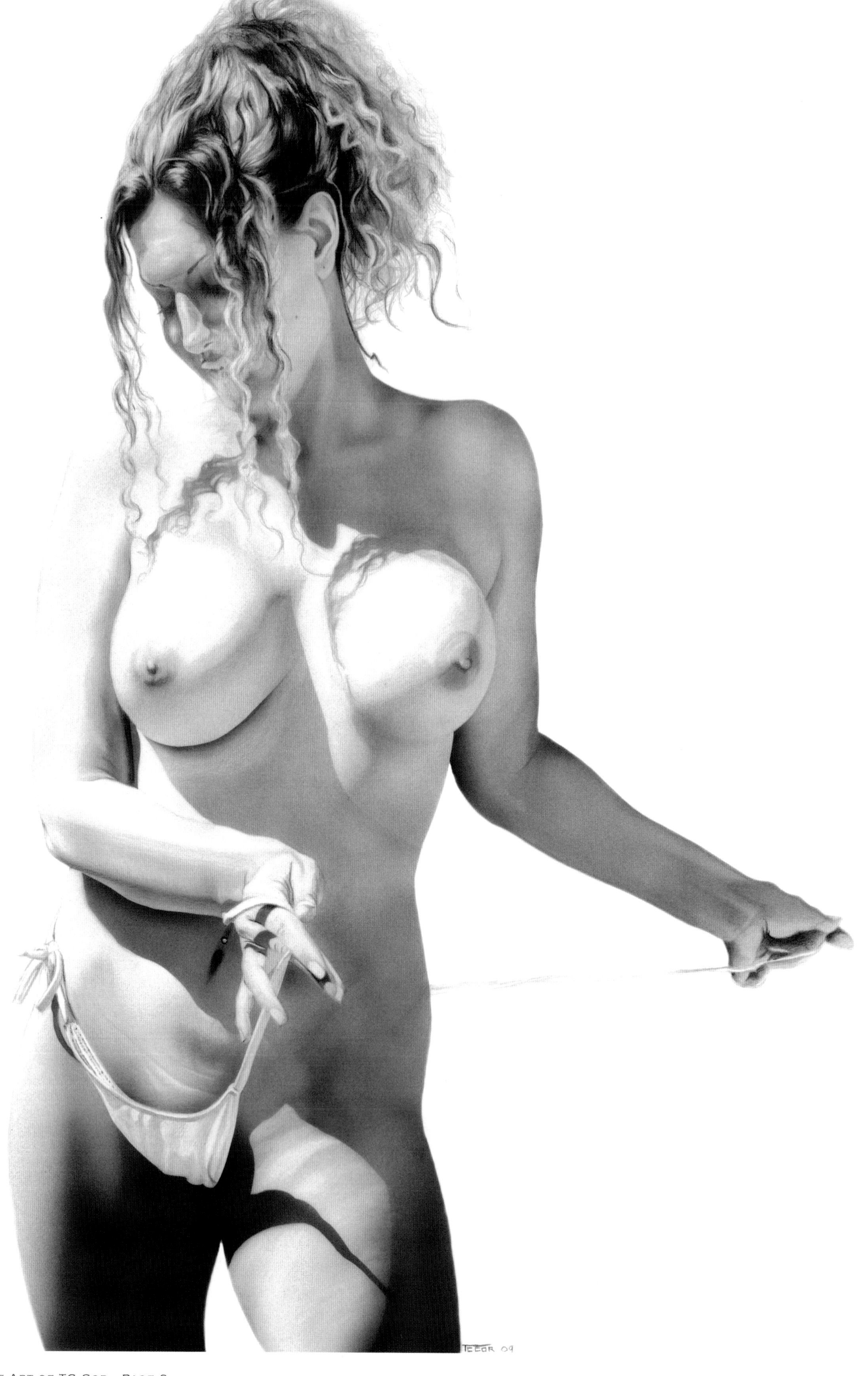

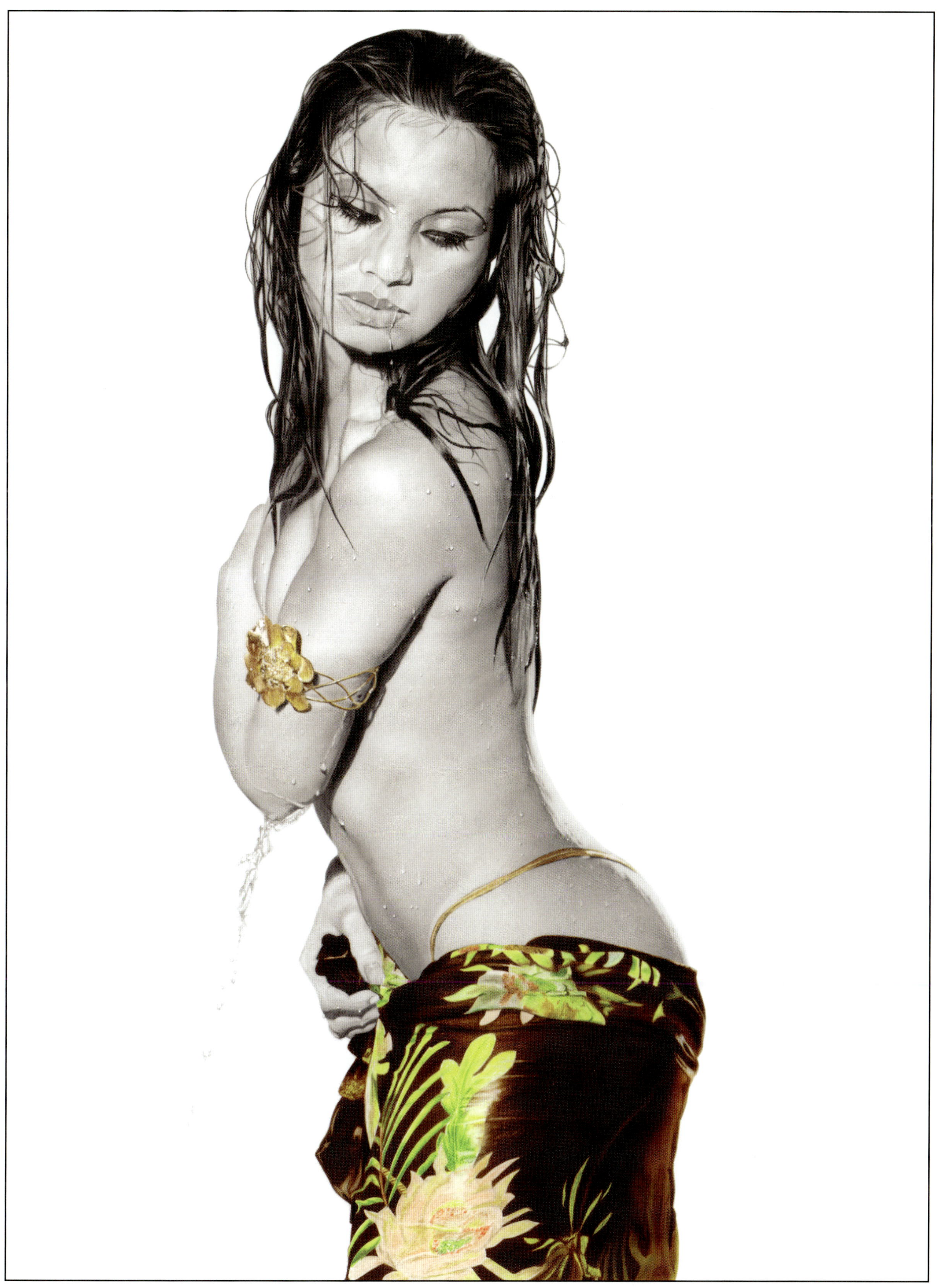

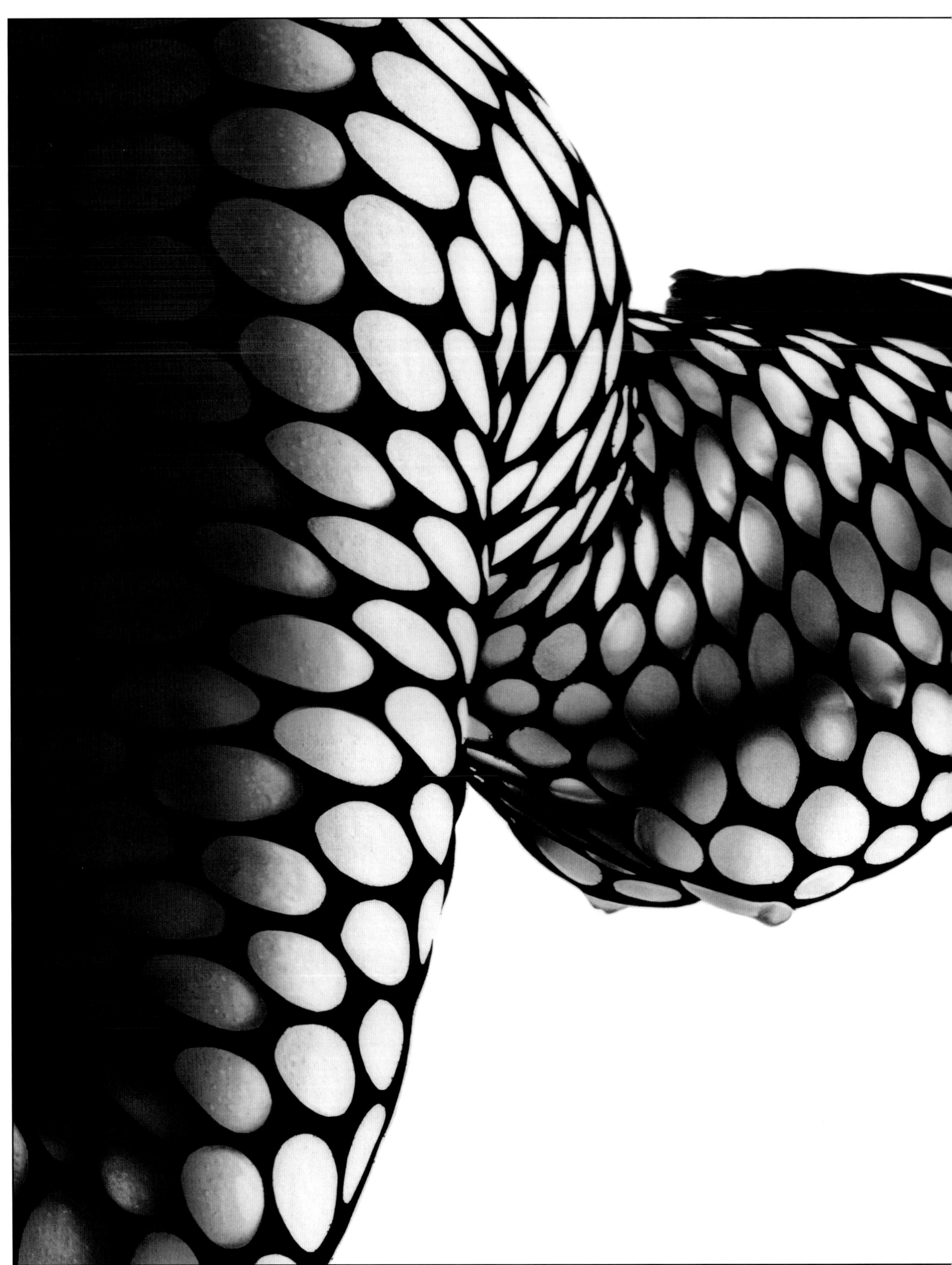

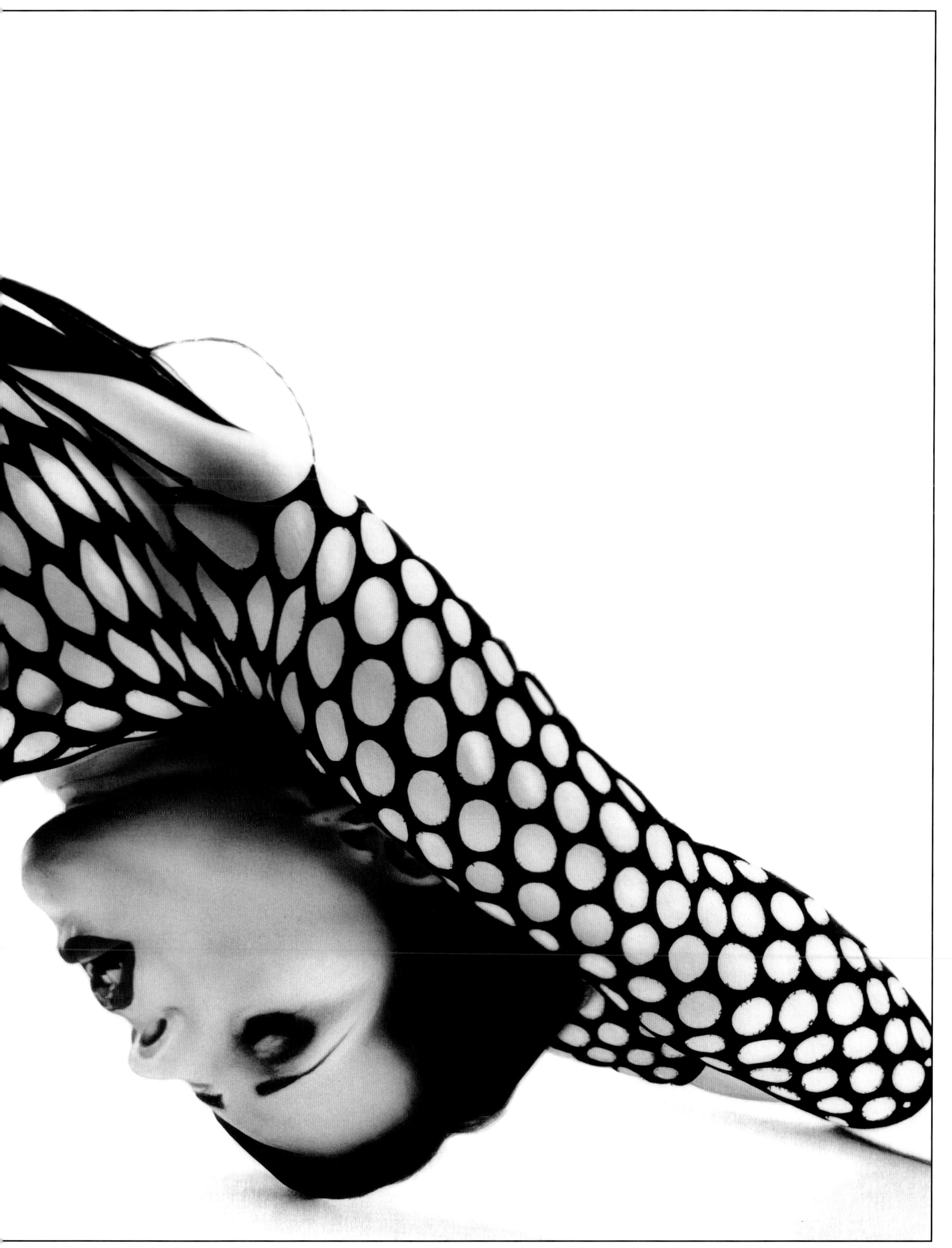

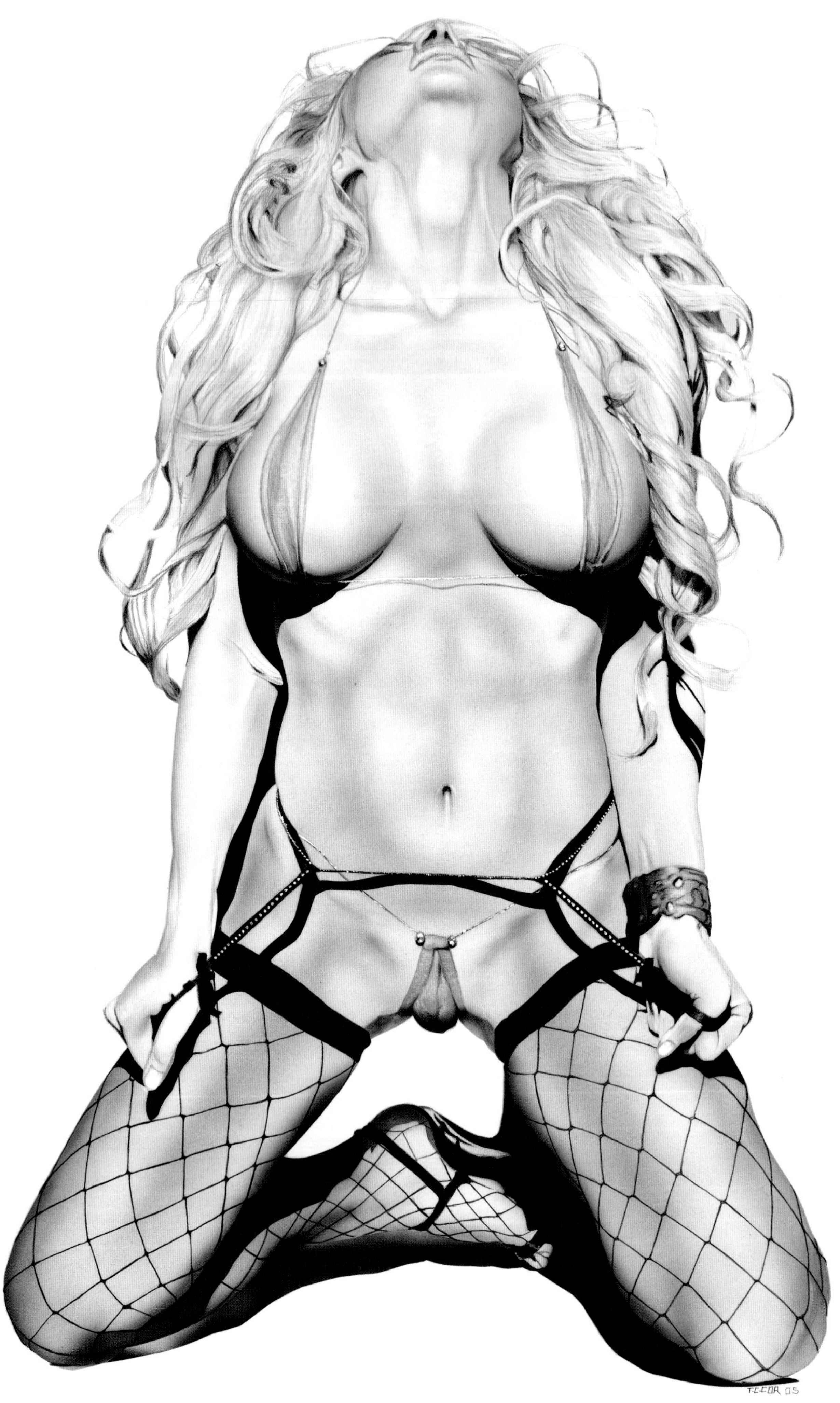
T.C.COR 05

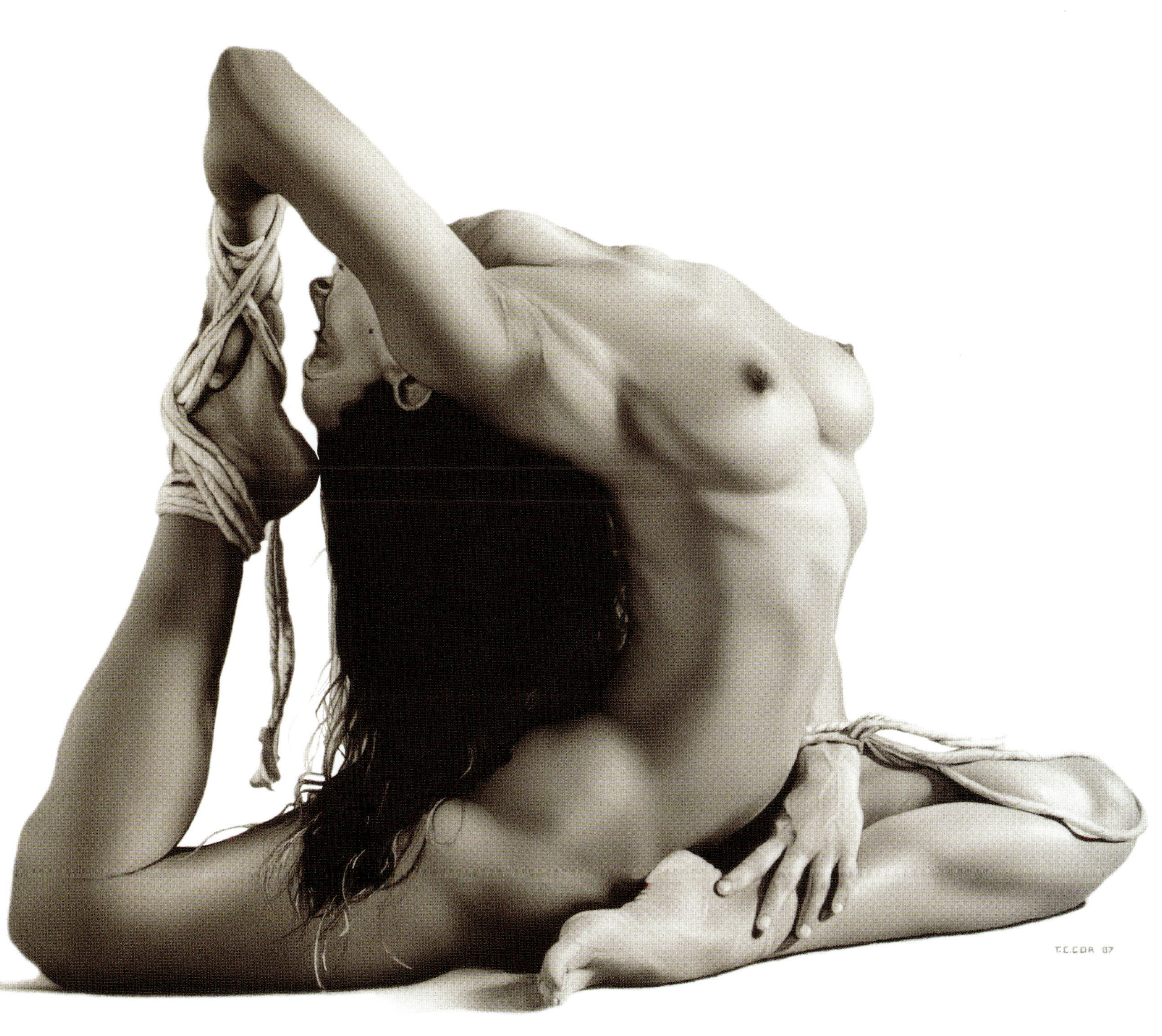
T.C.COR 07

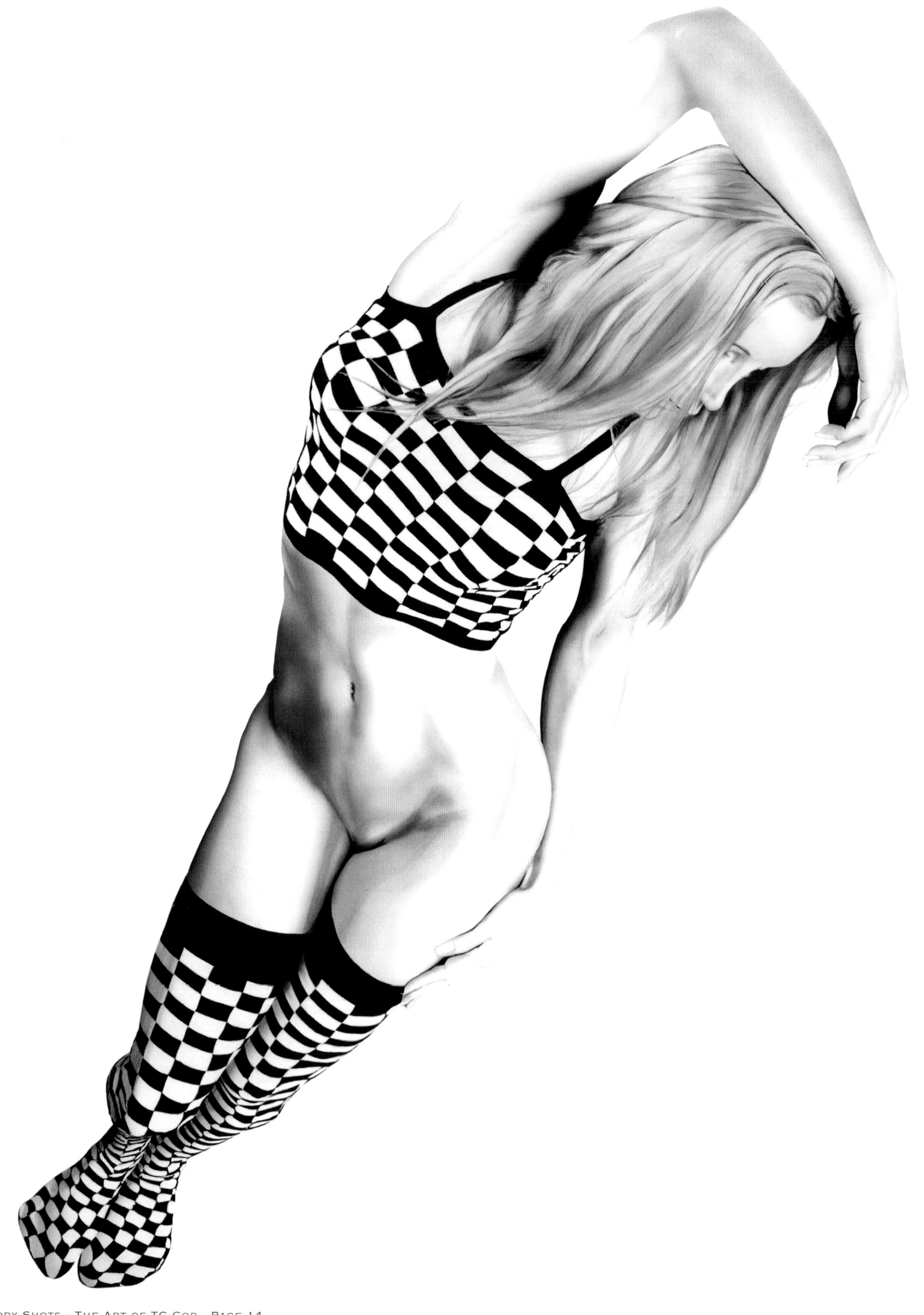

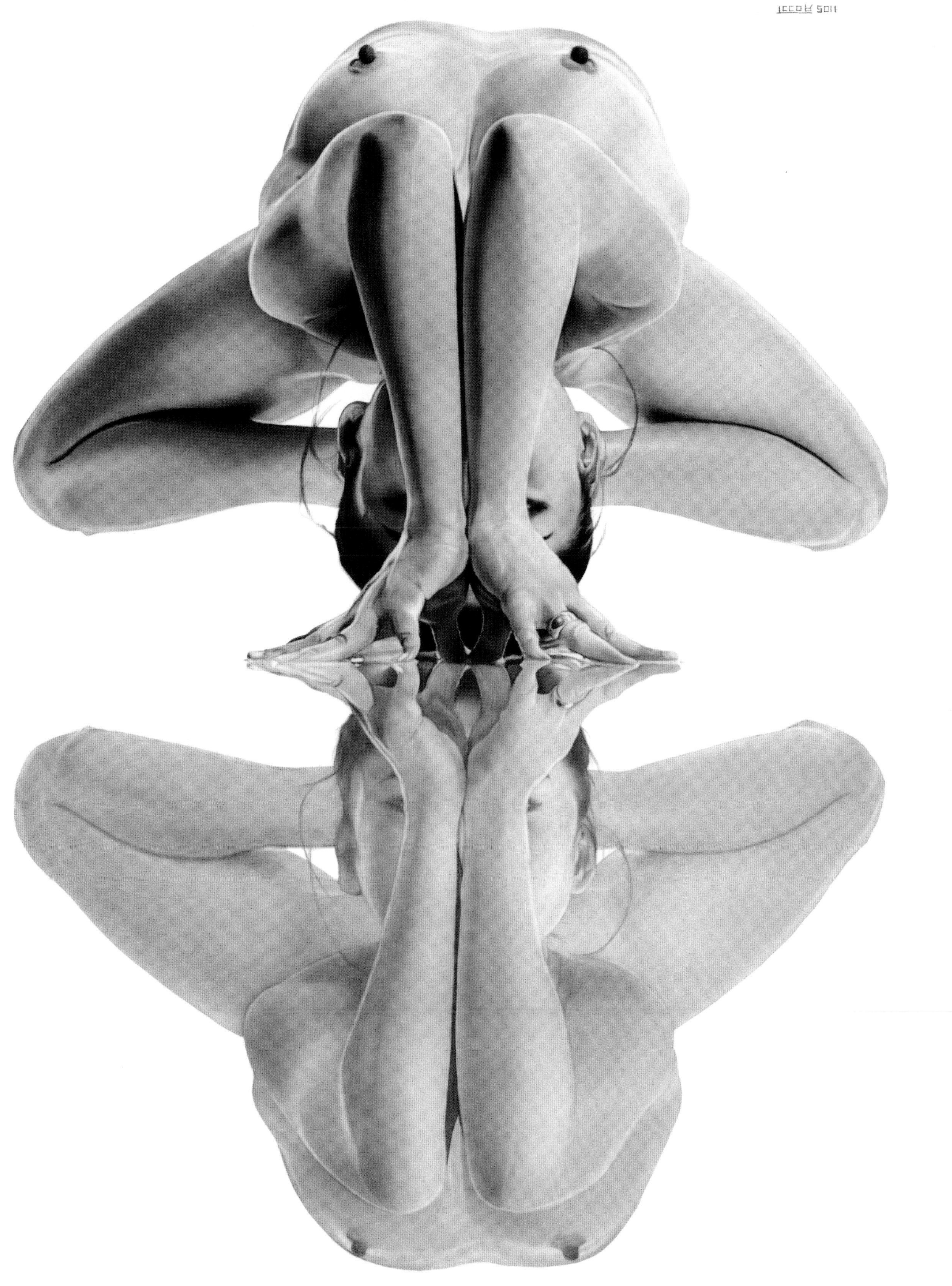
TECOR 2011

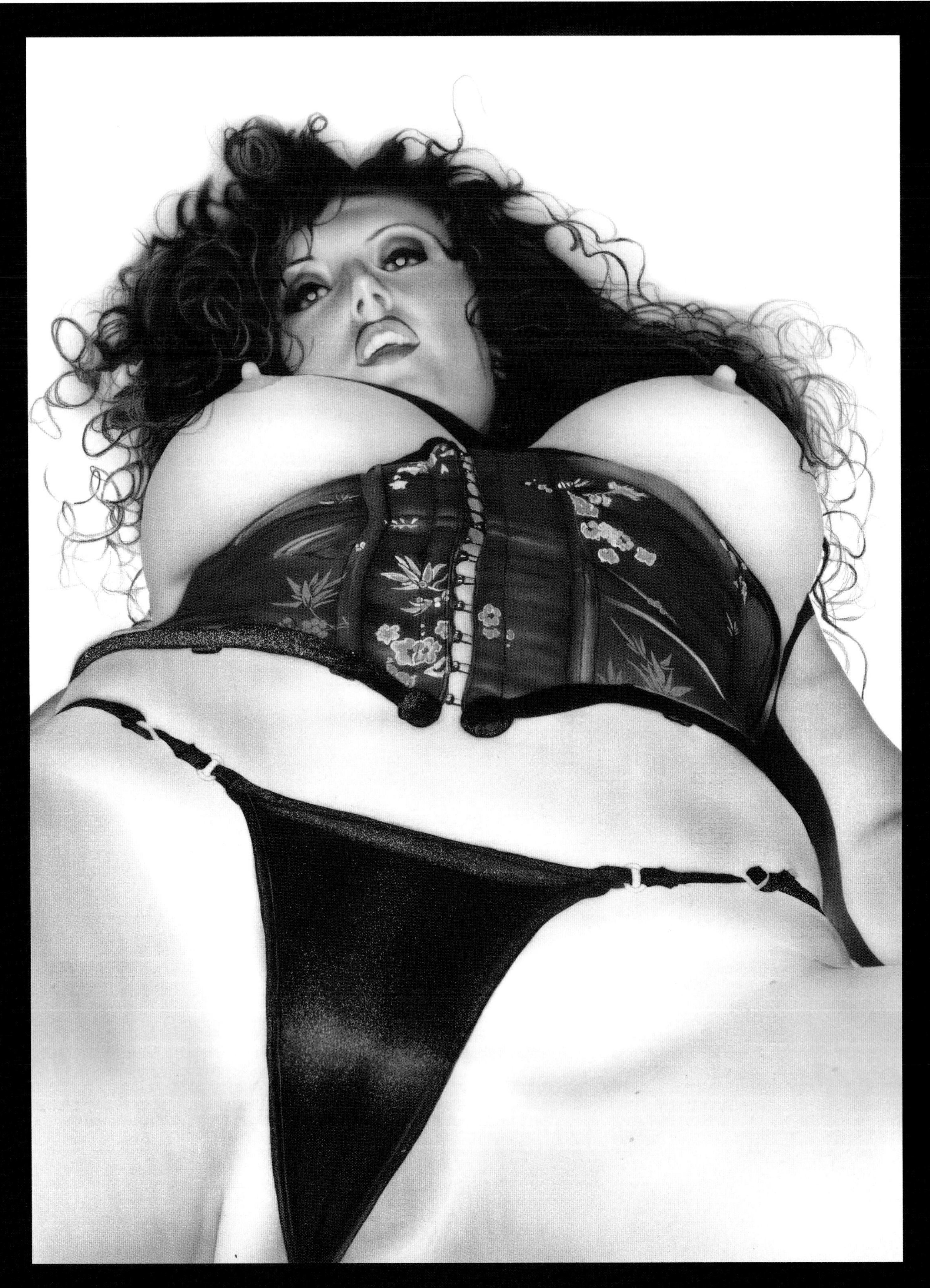

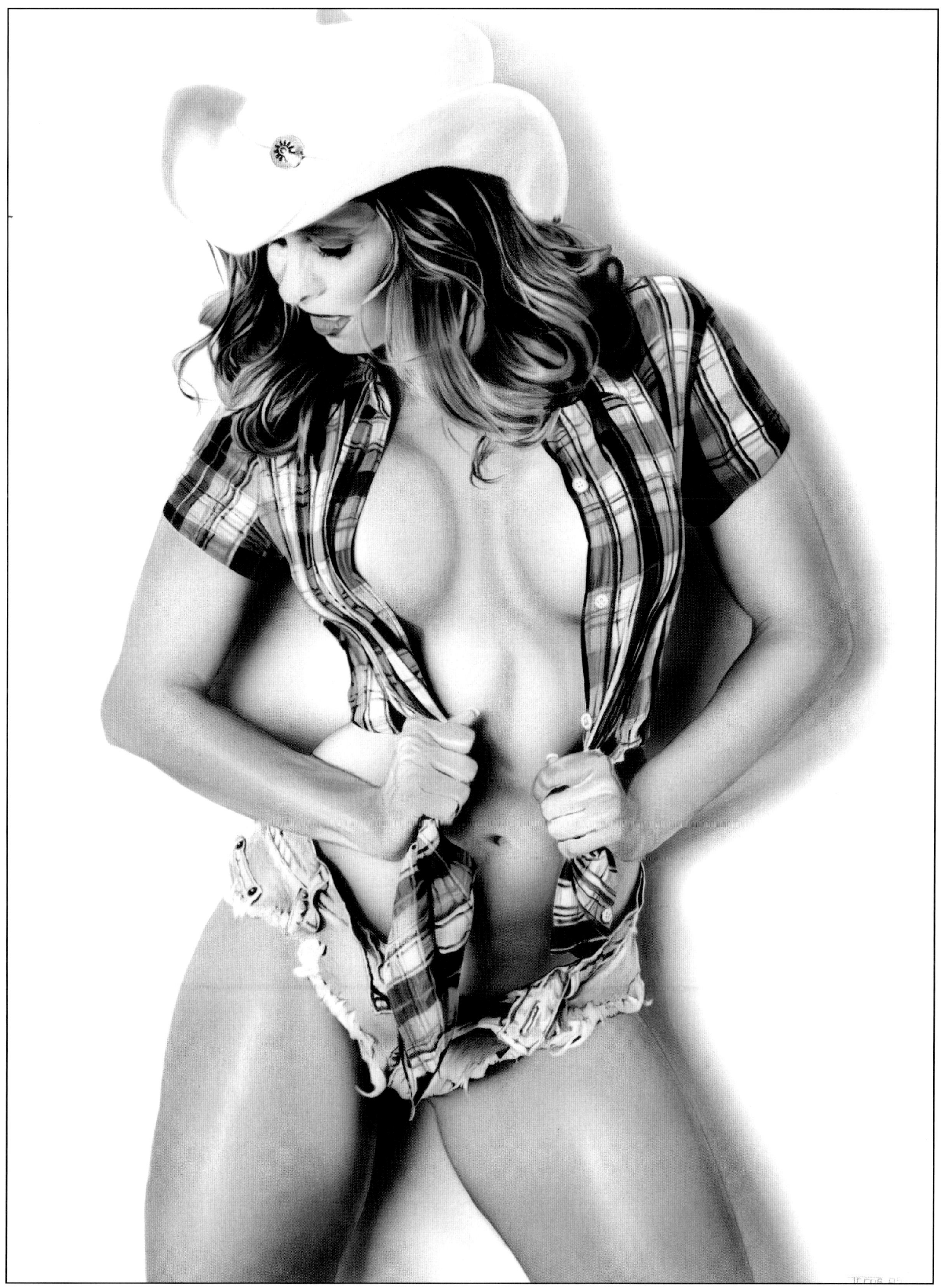

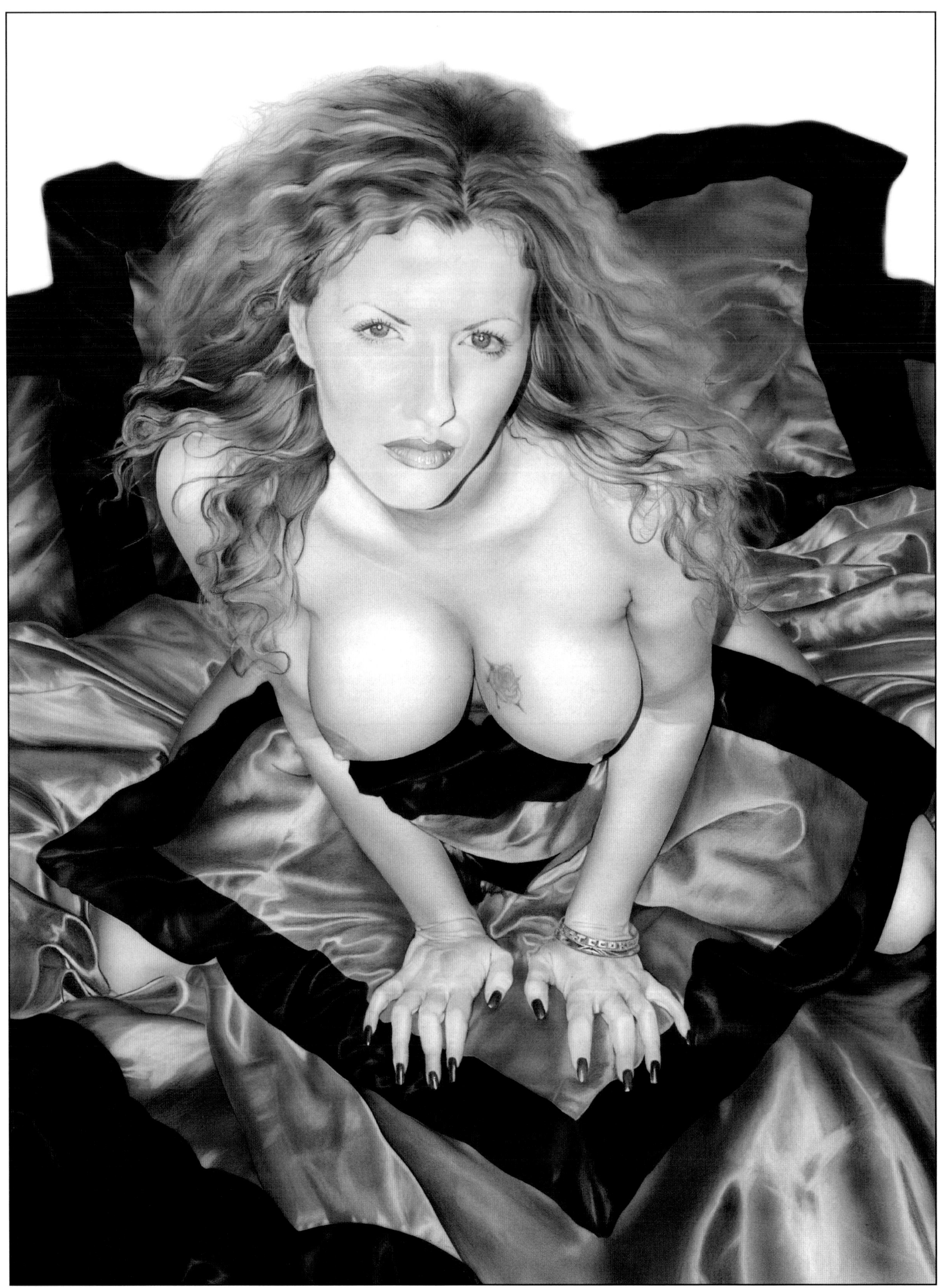

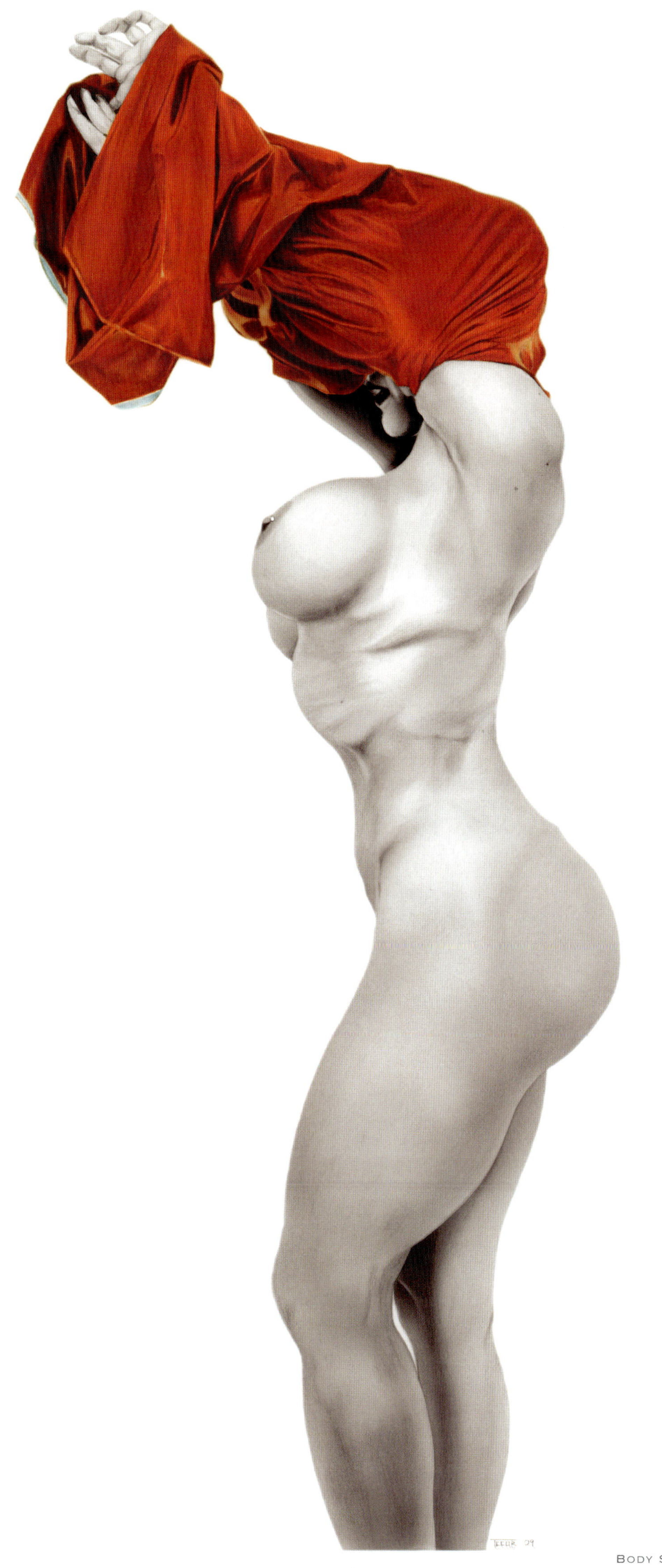

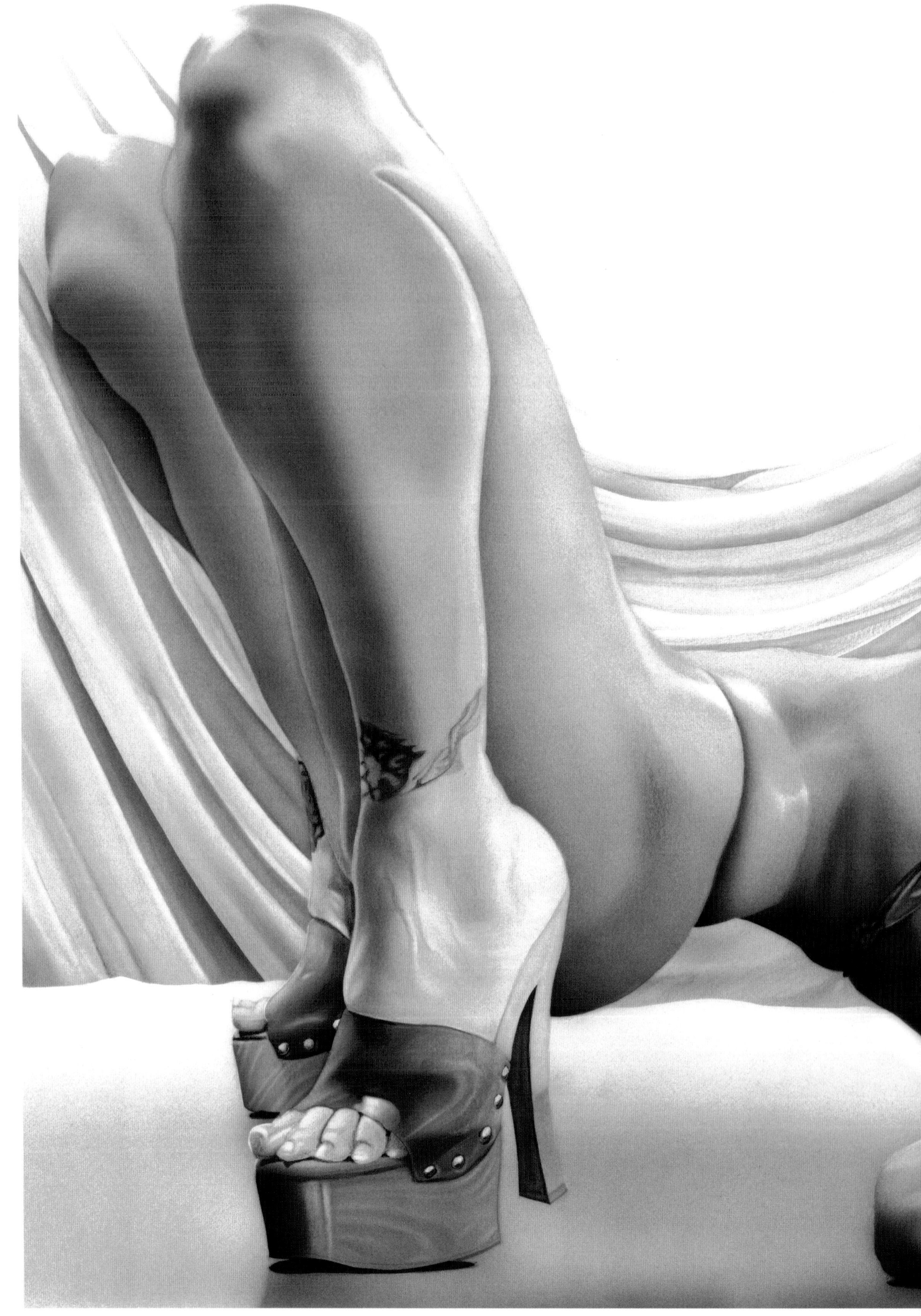

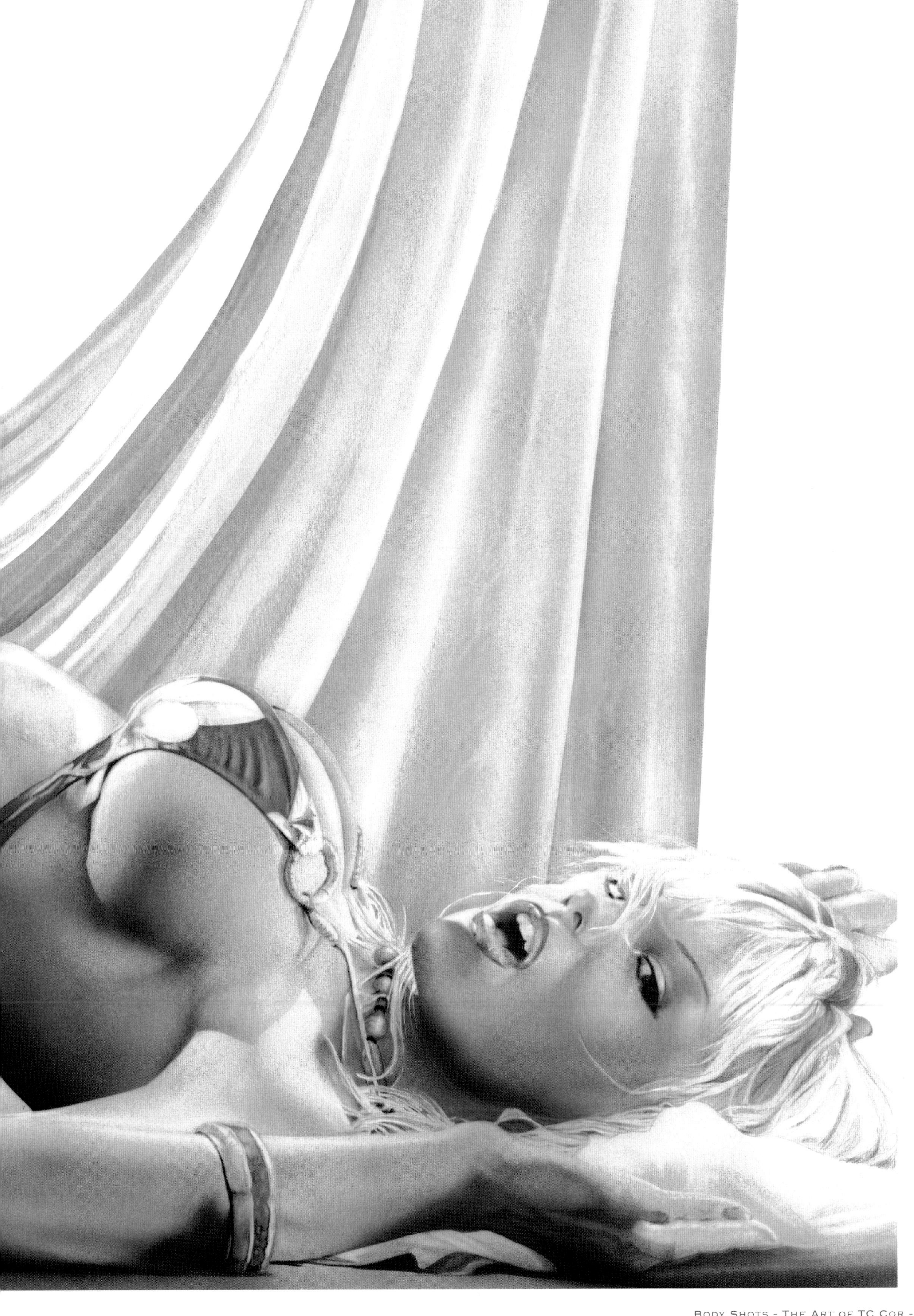

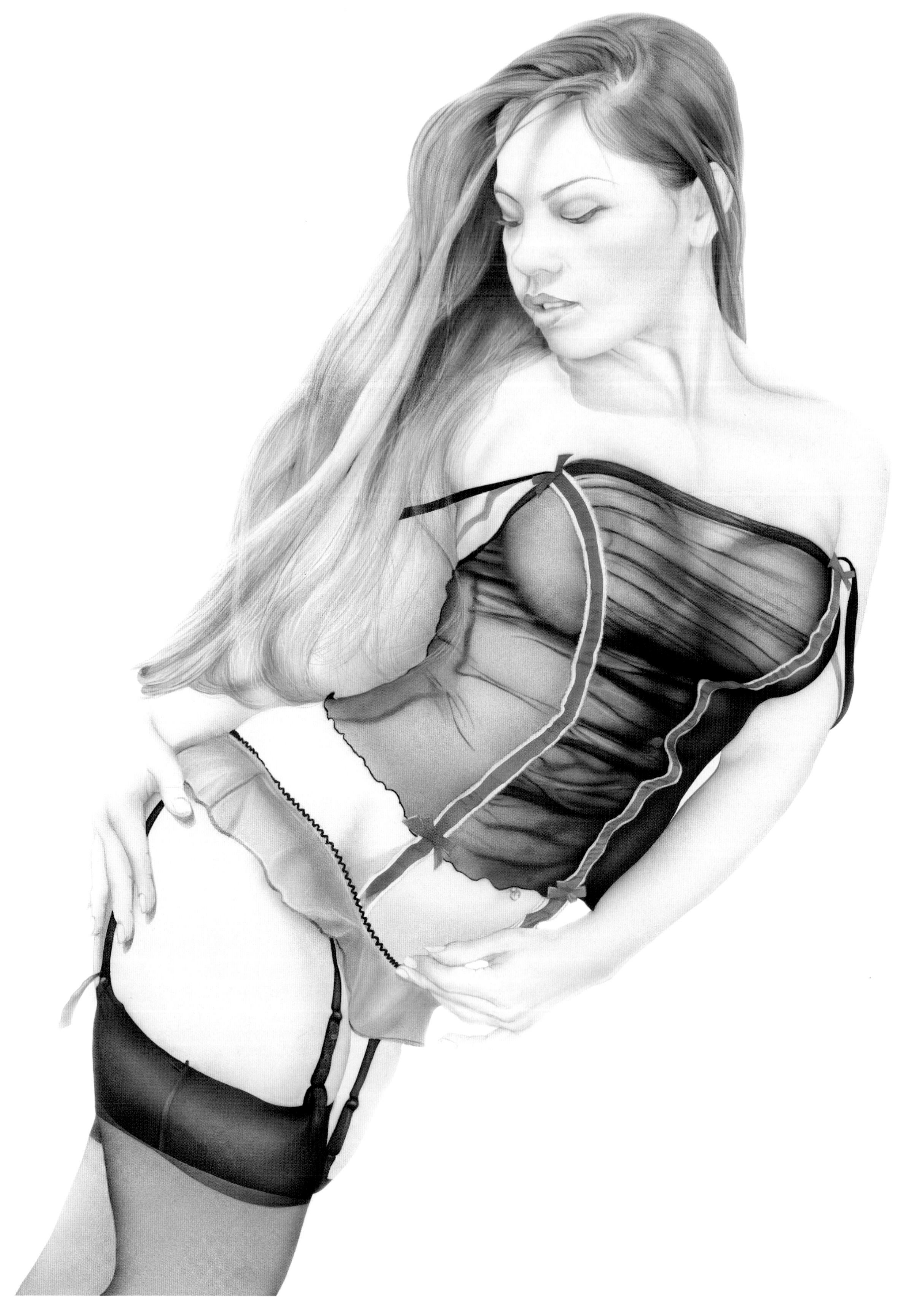

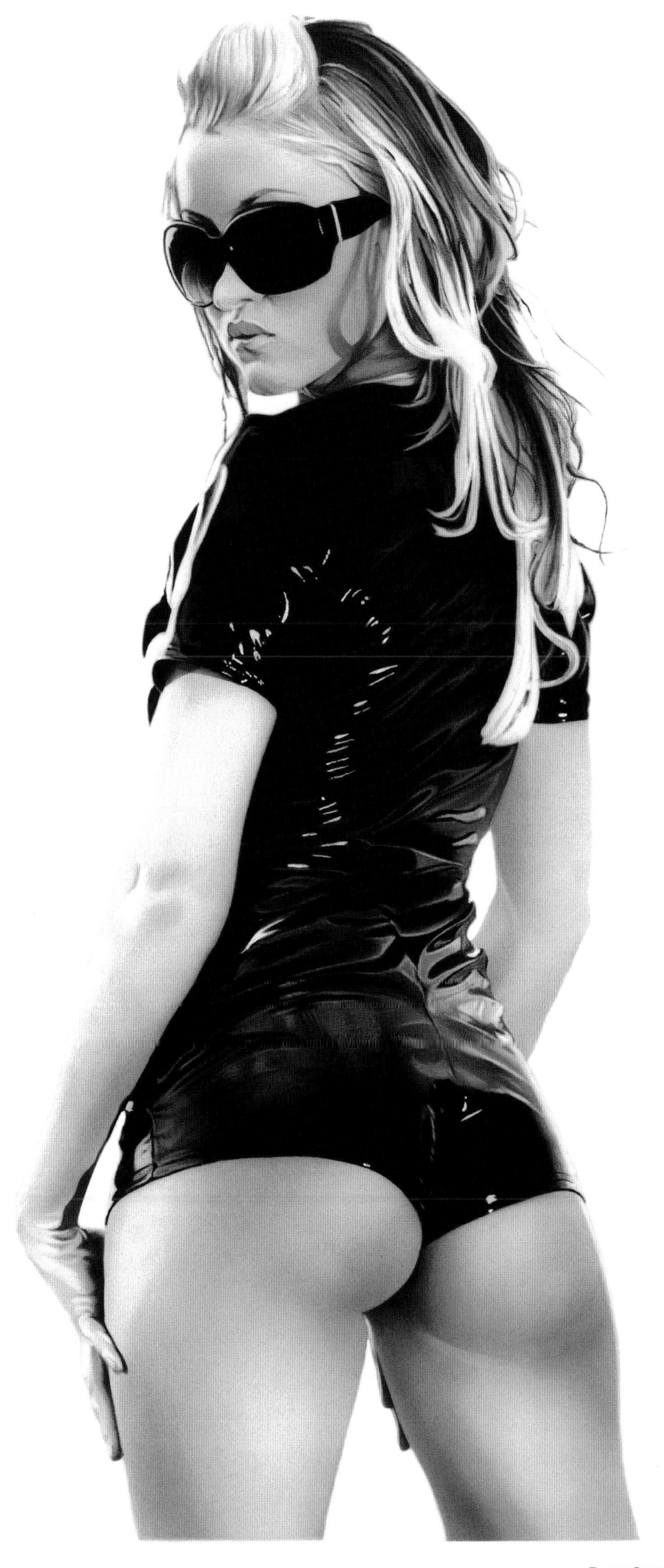

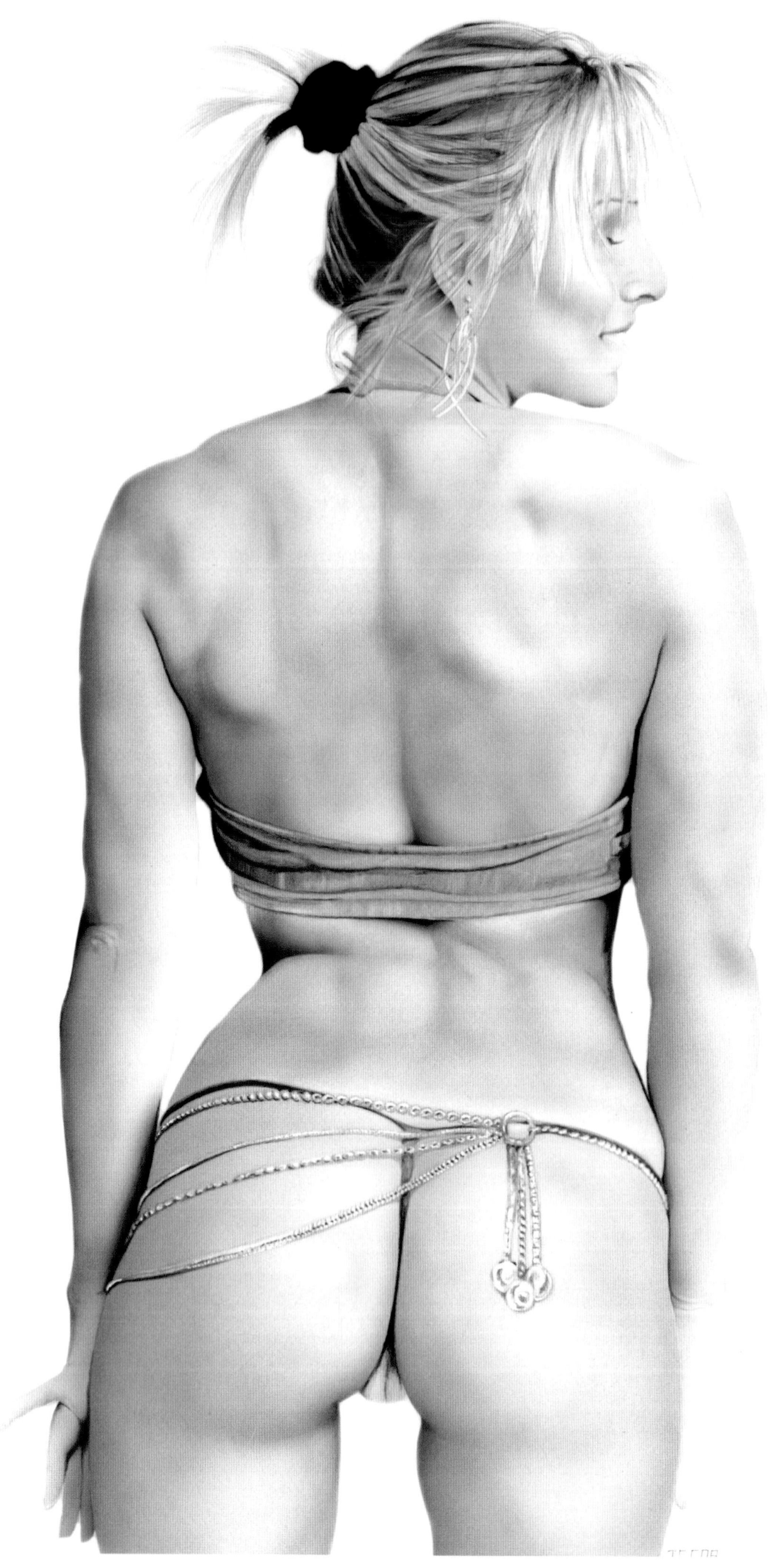

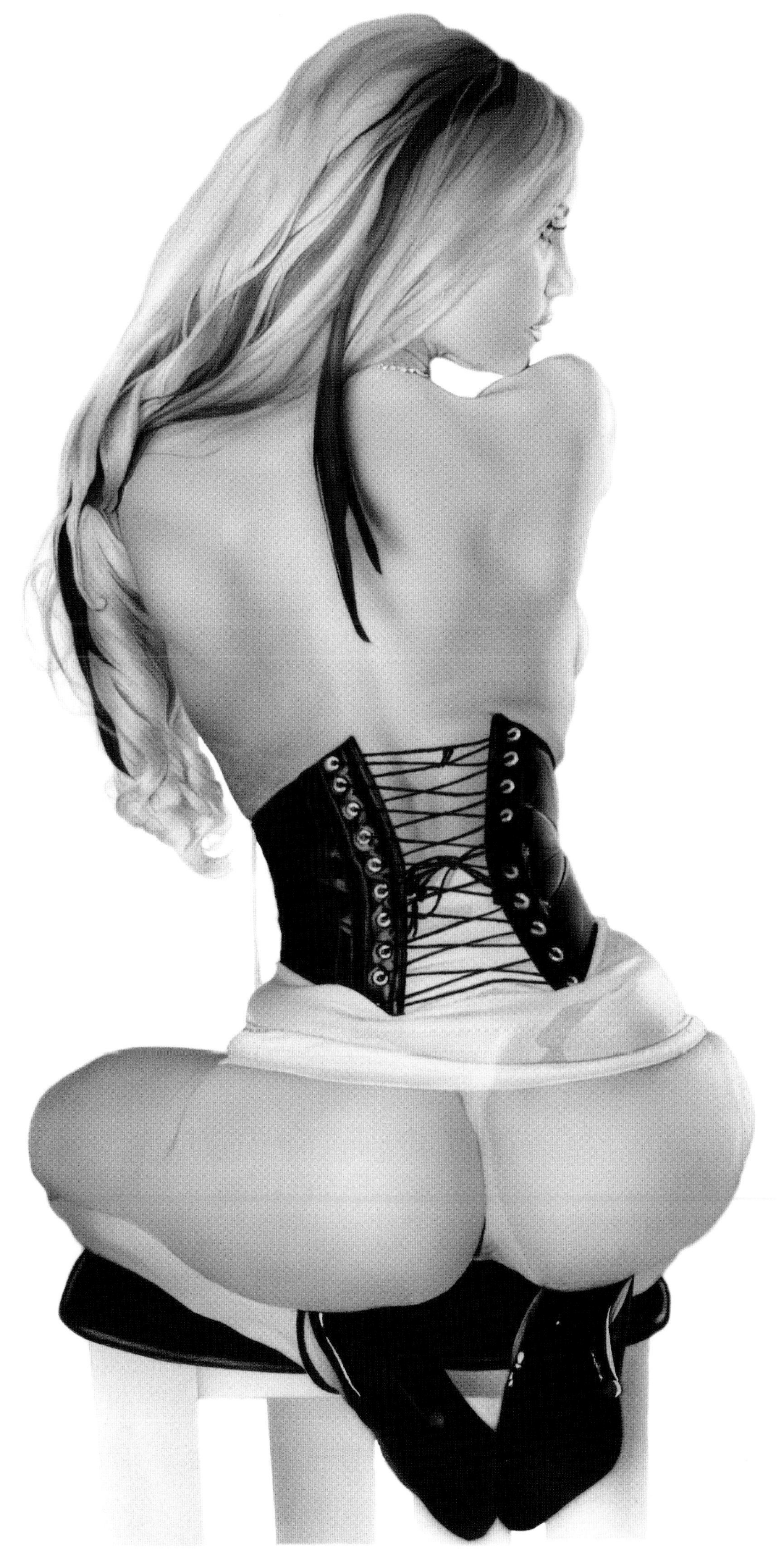

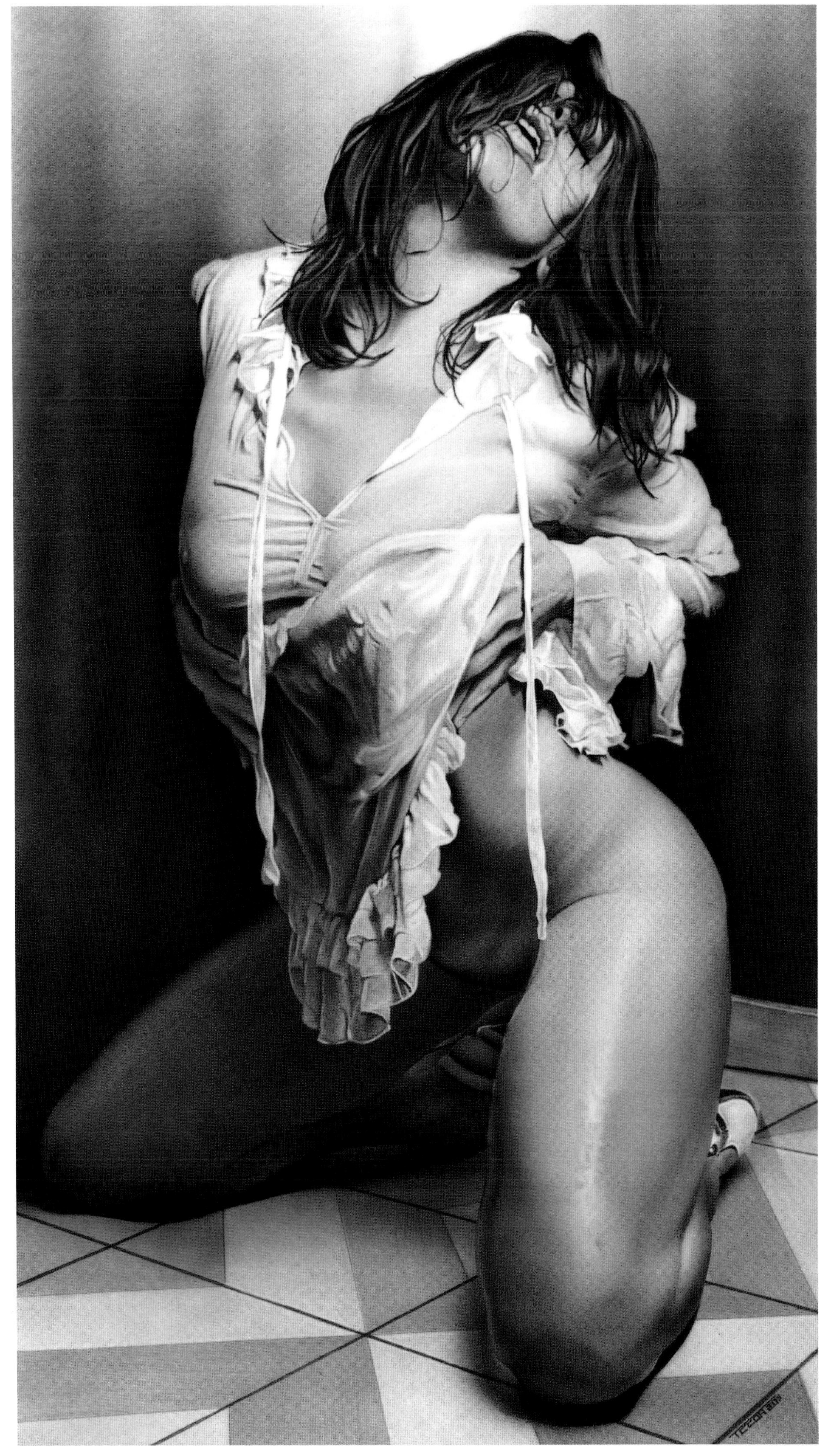

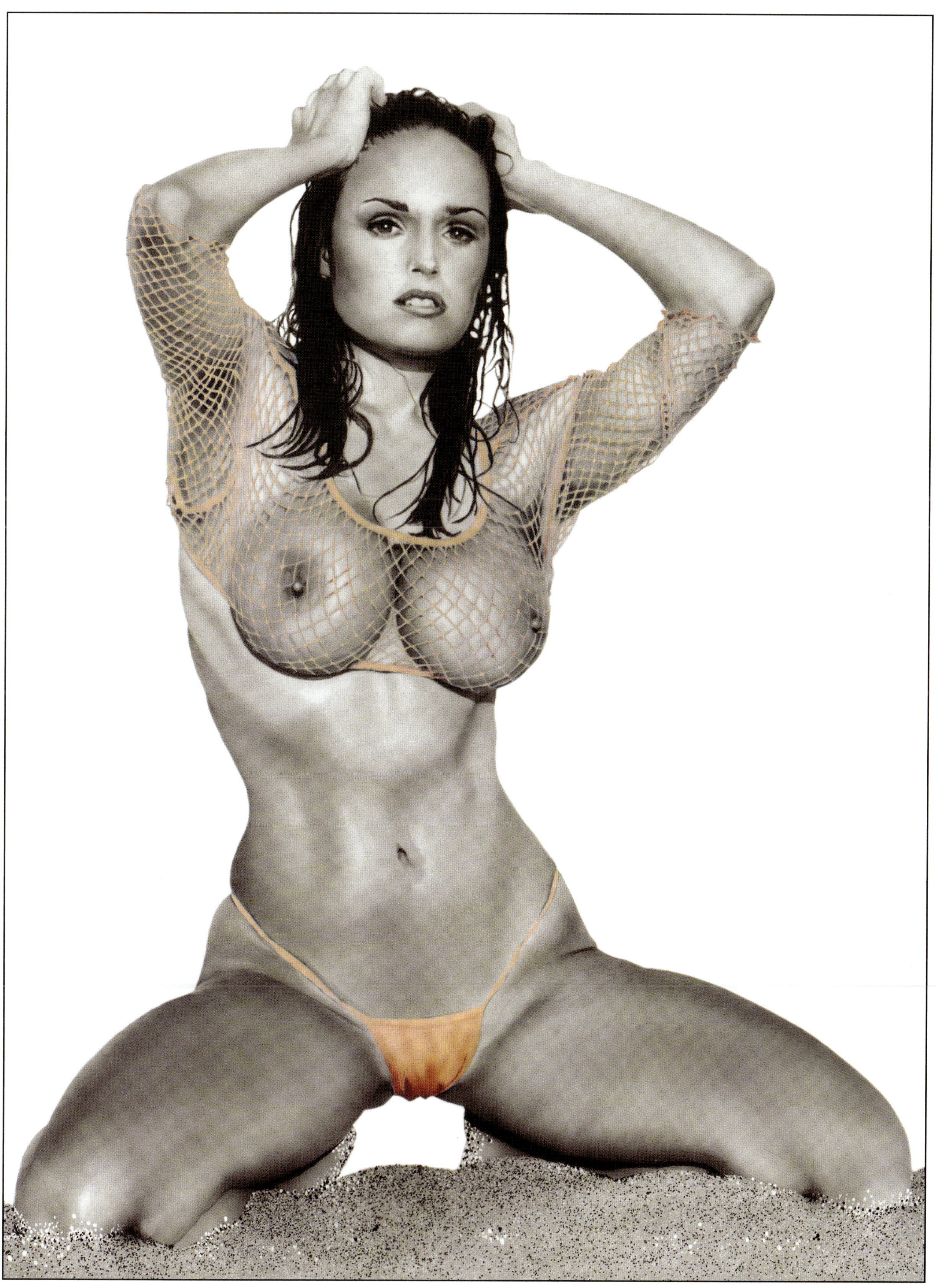

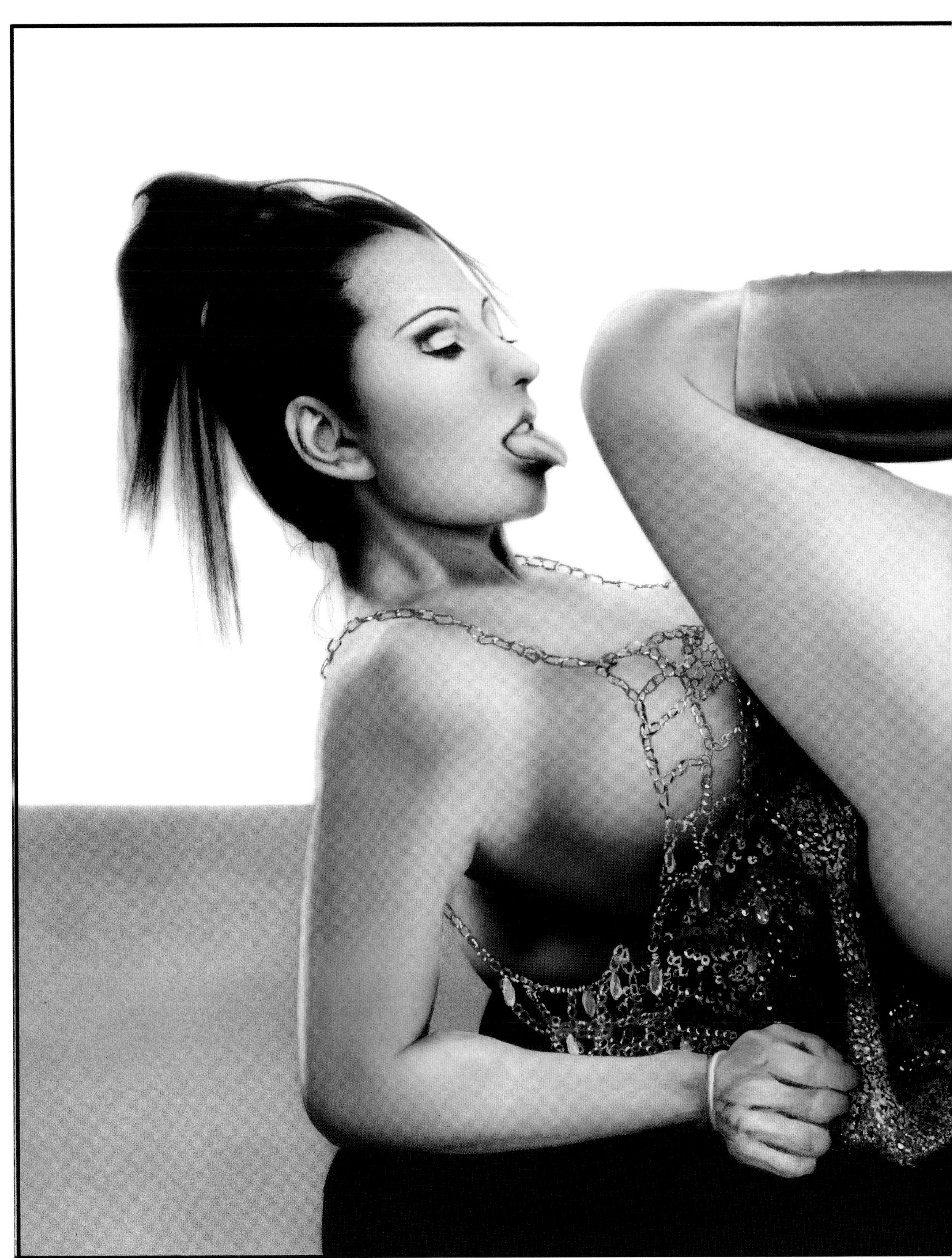

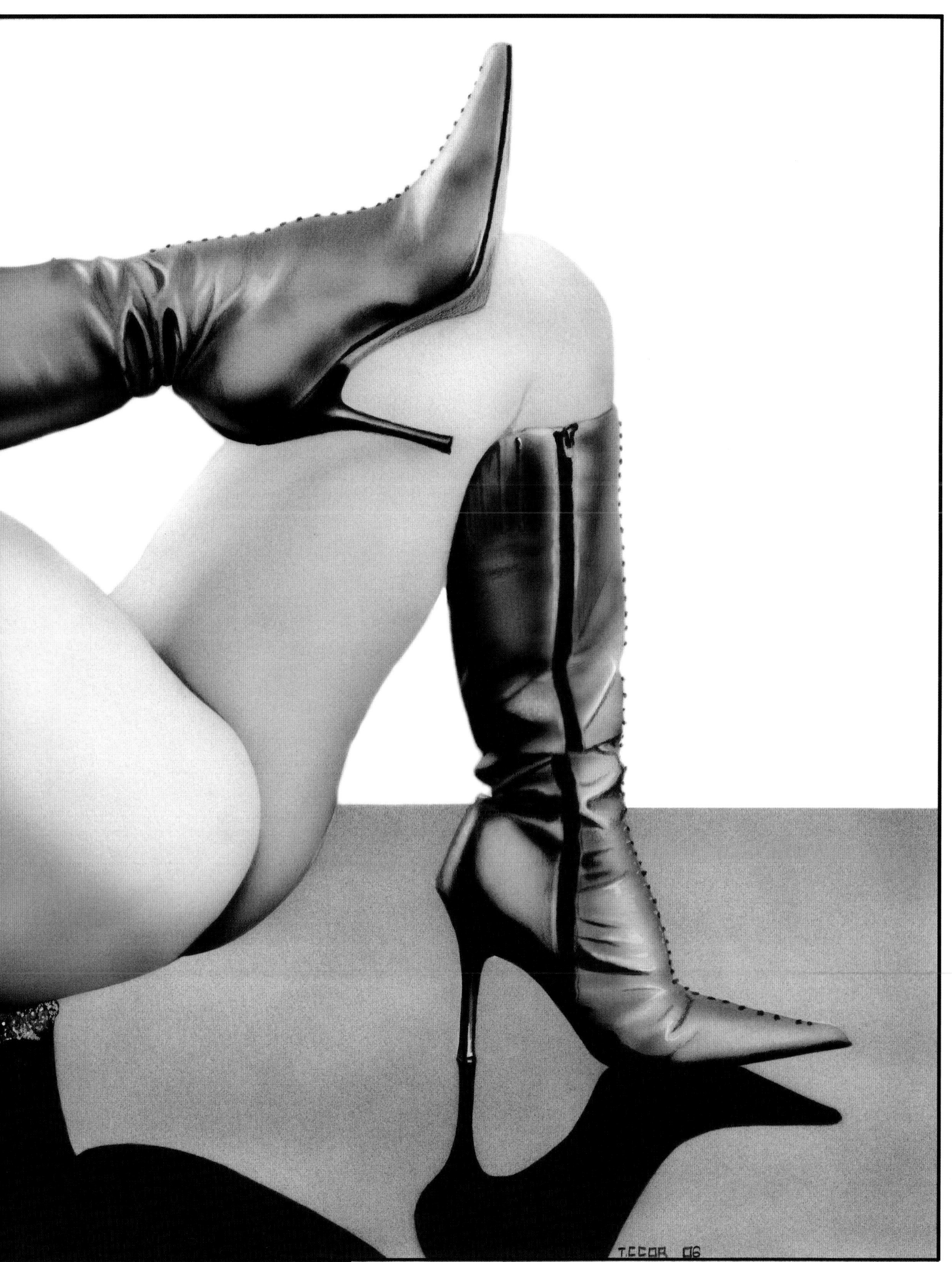
T.C.COR 06

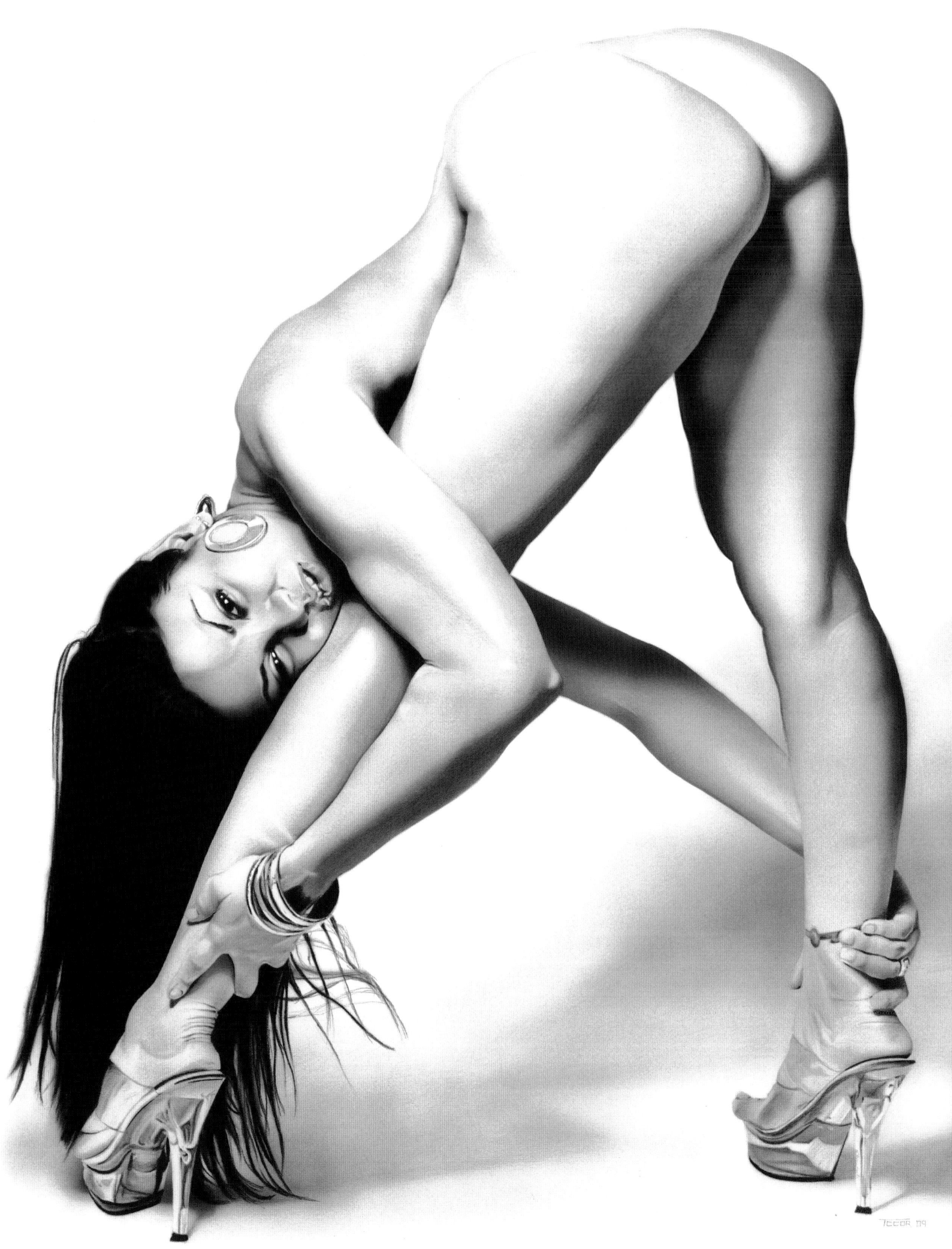

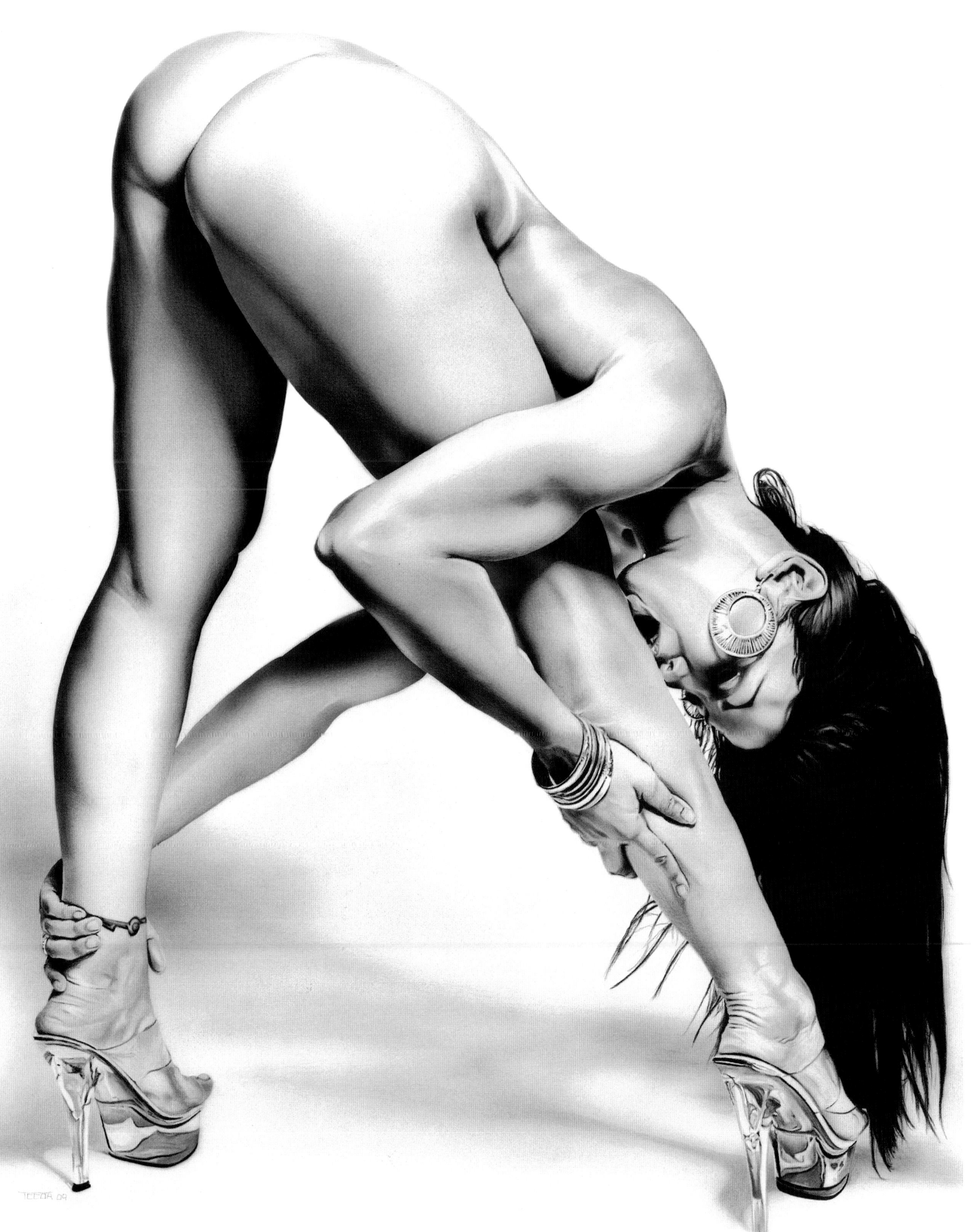

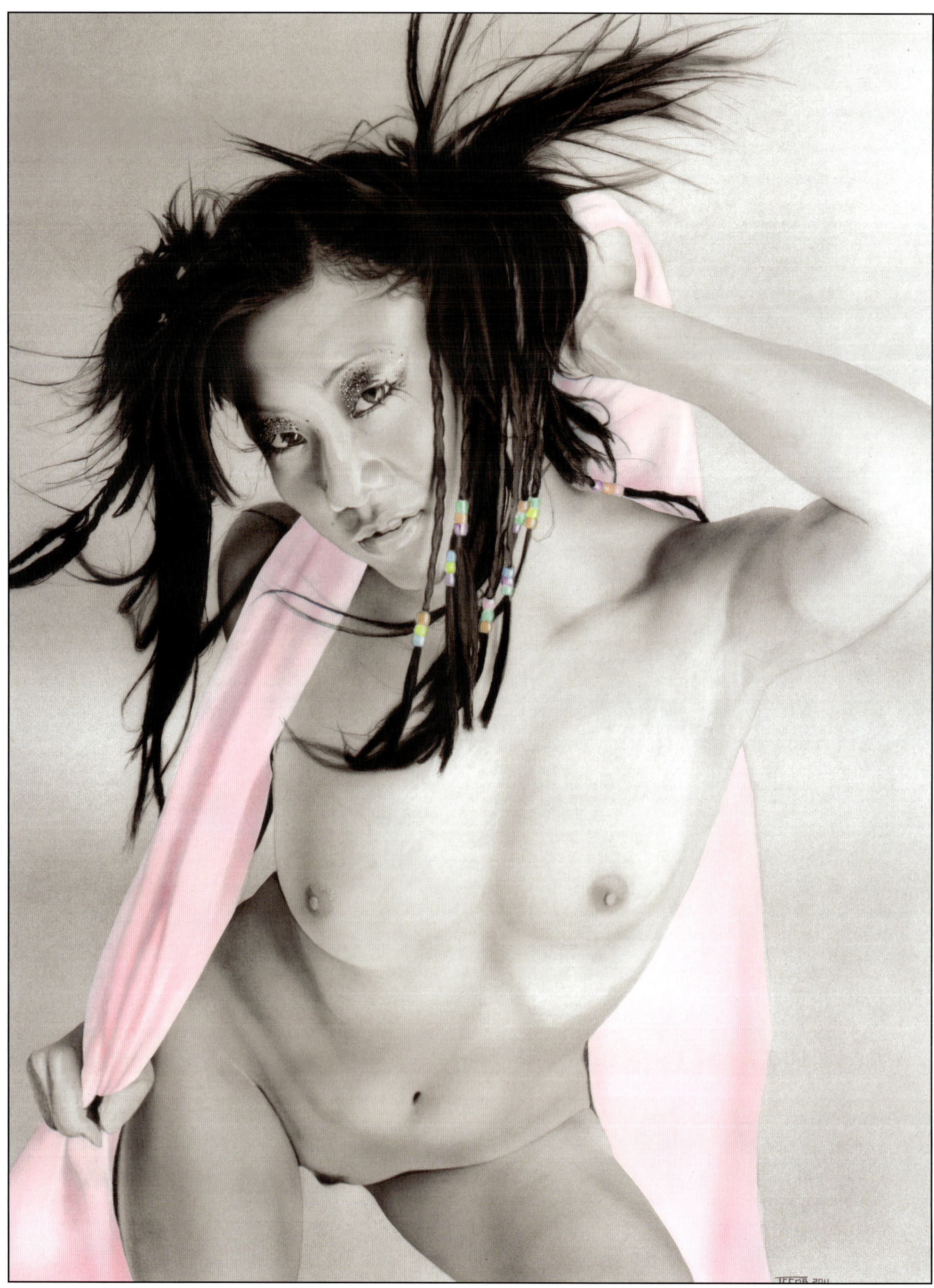

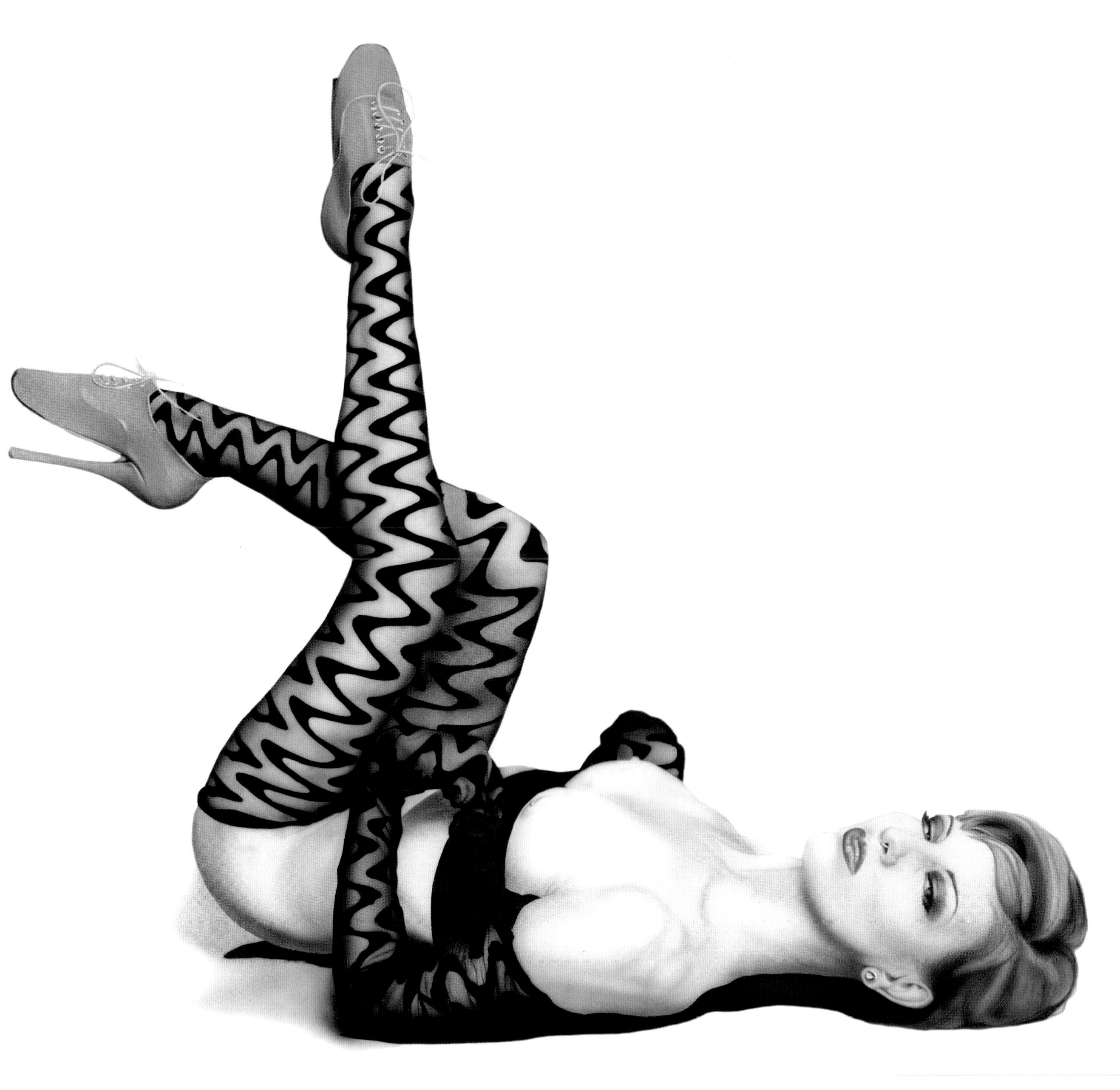

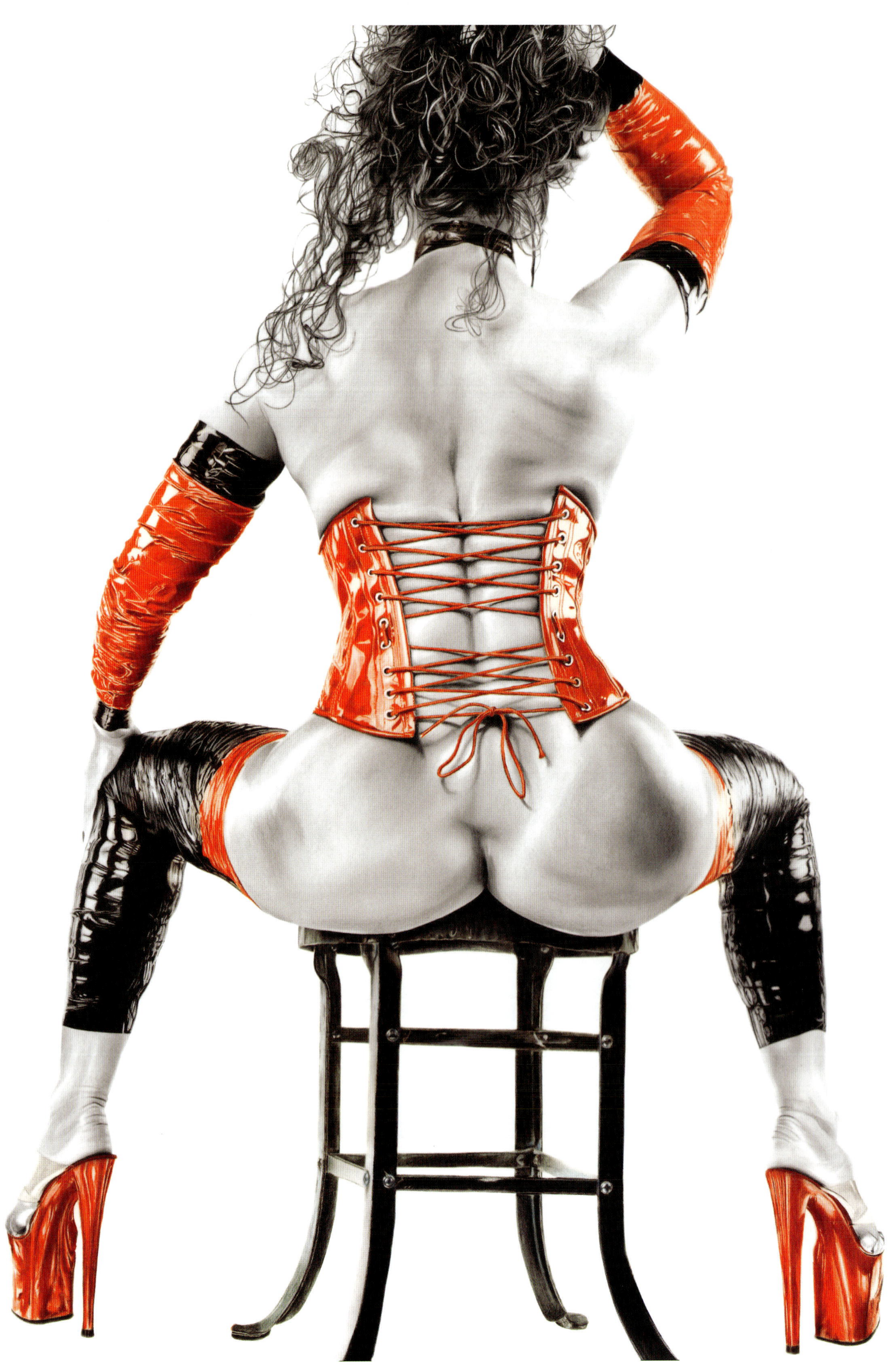

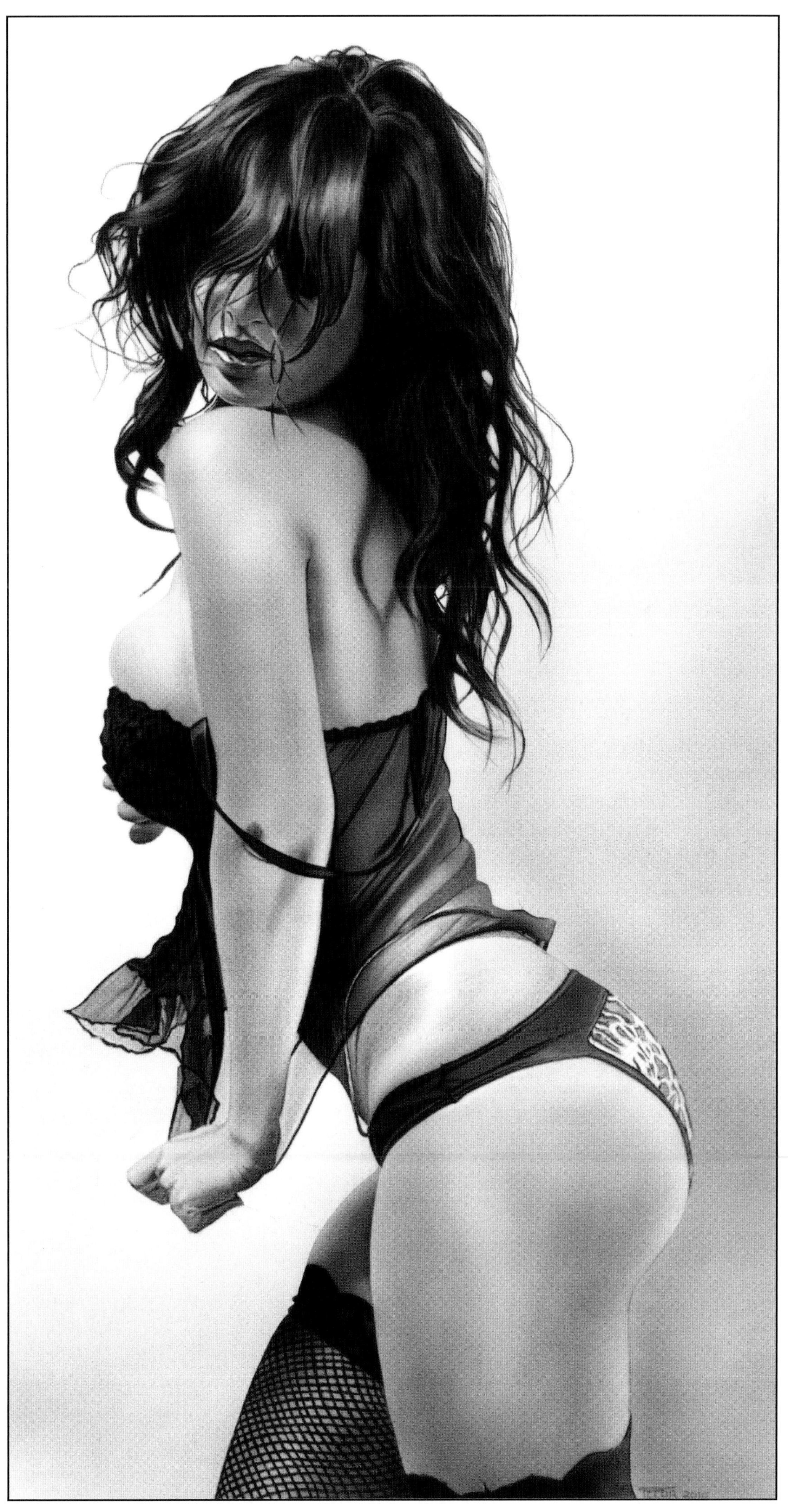

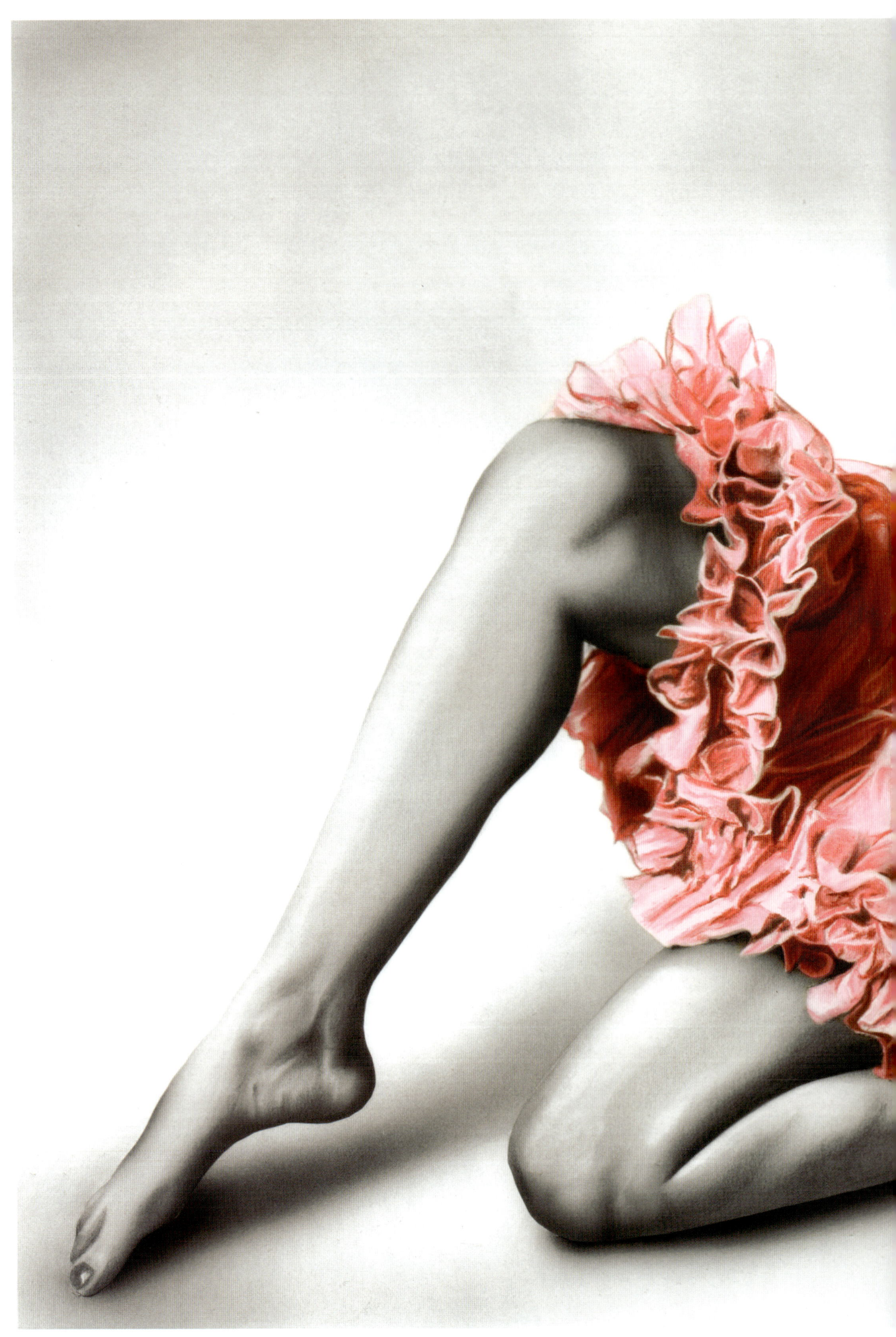

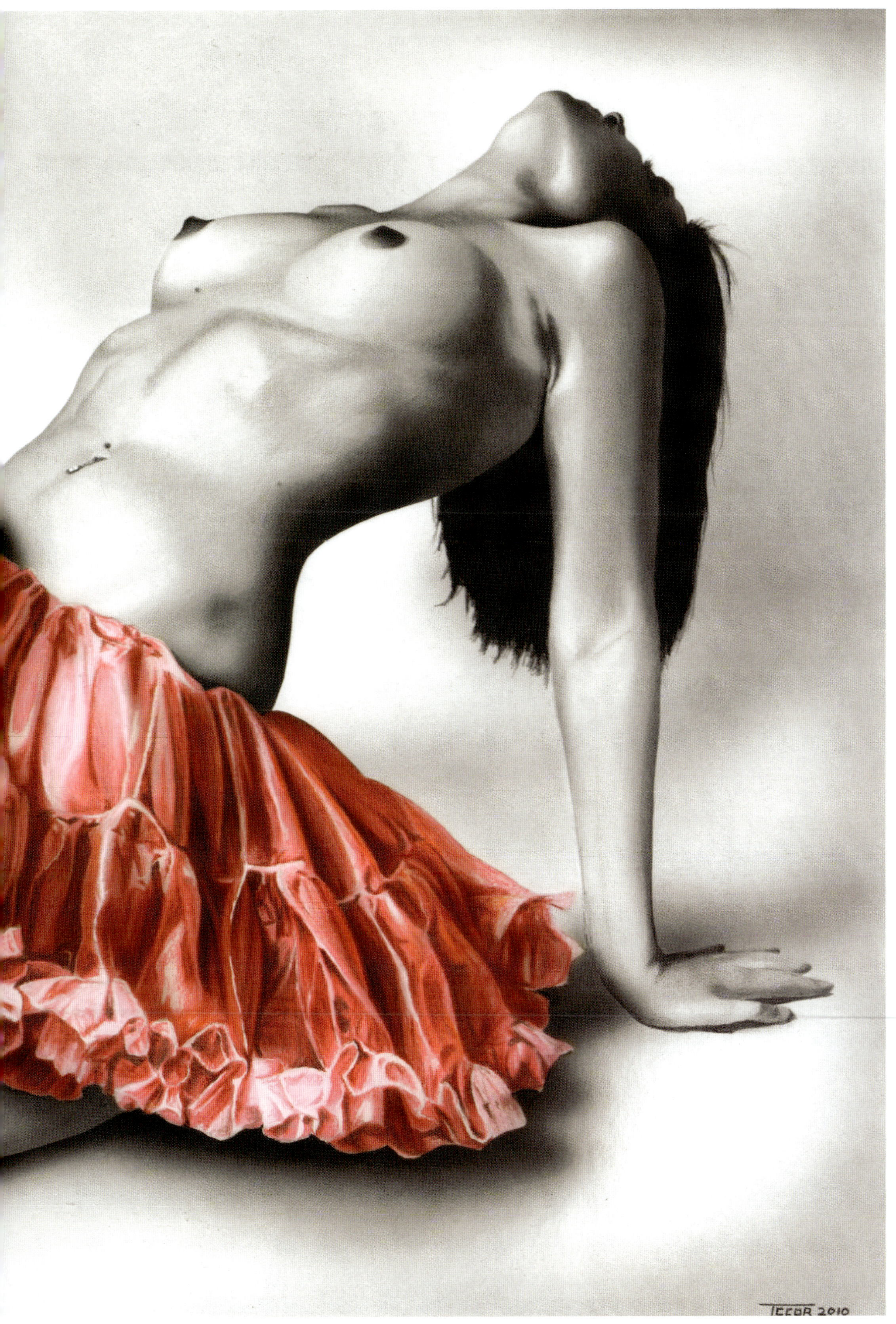
TCCOR 2010

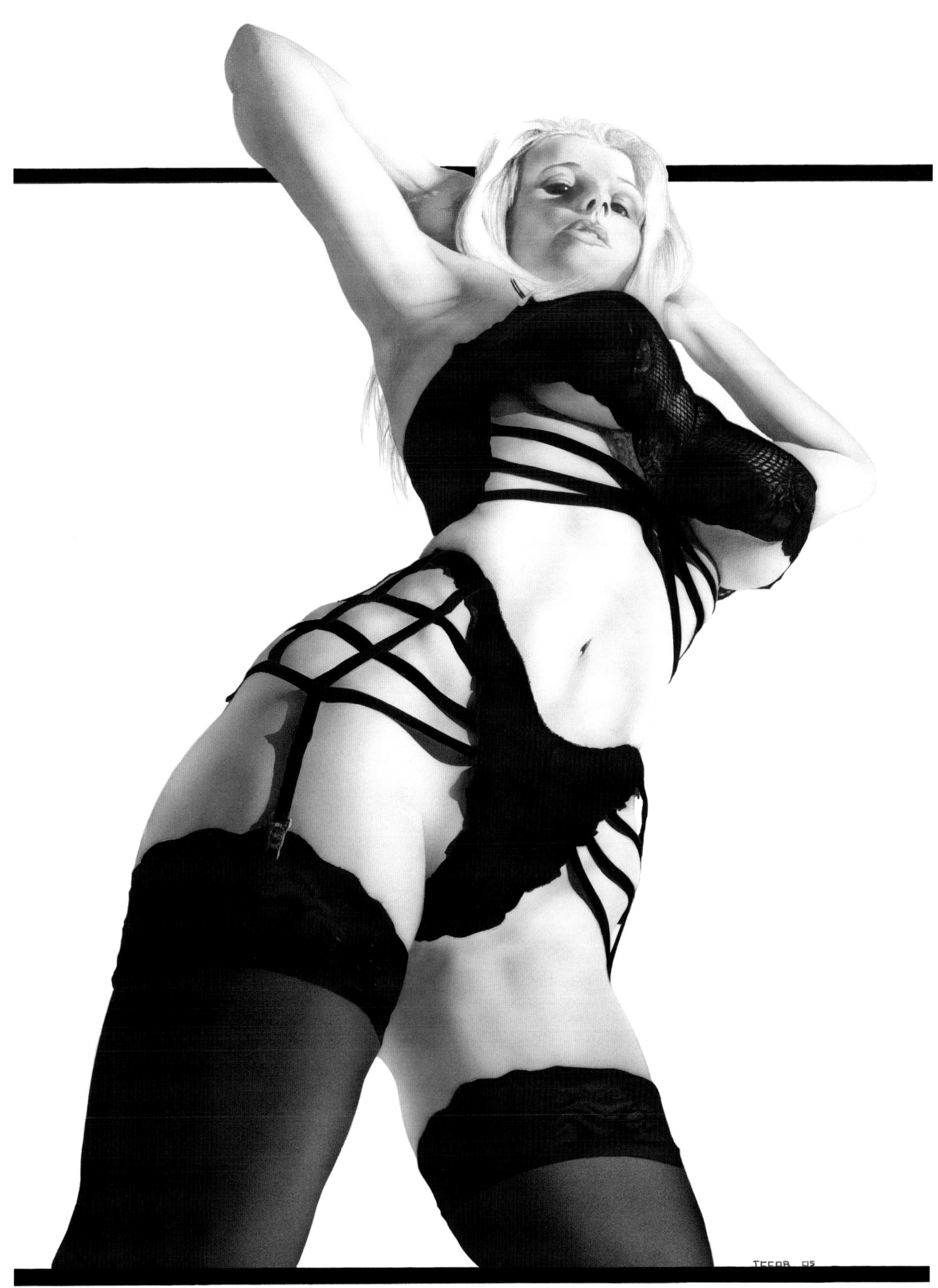

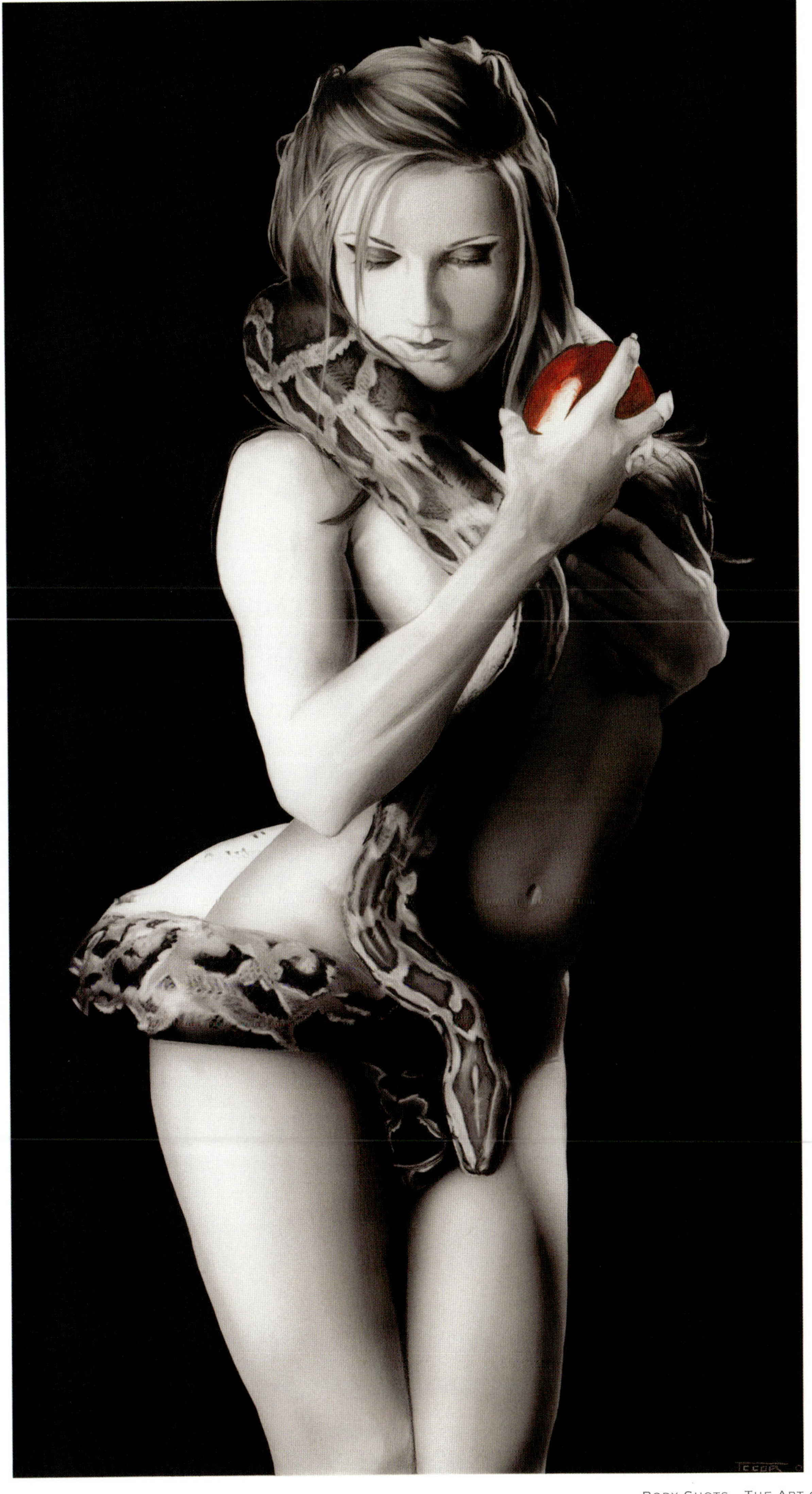

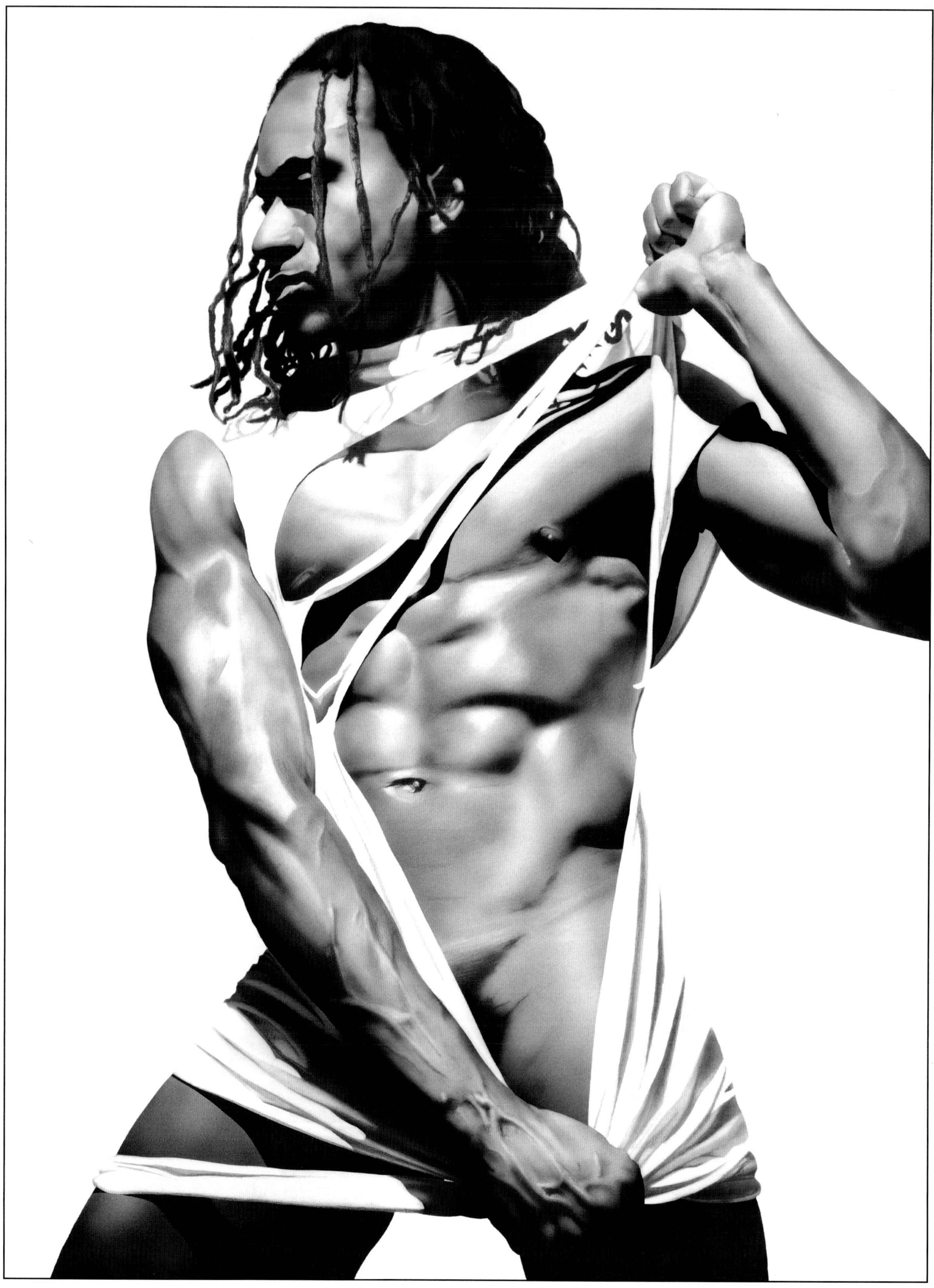

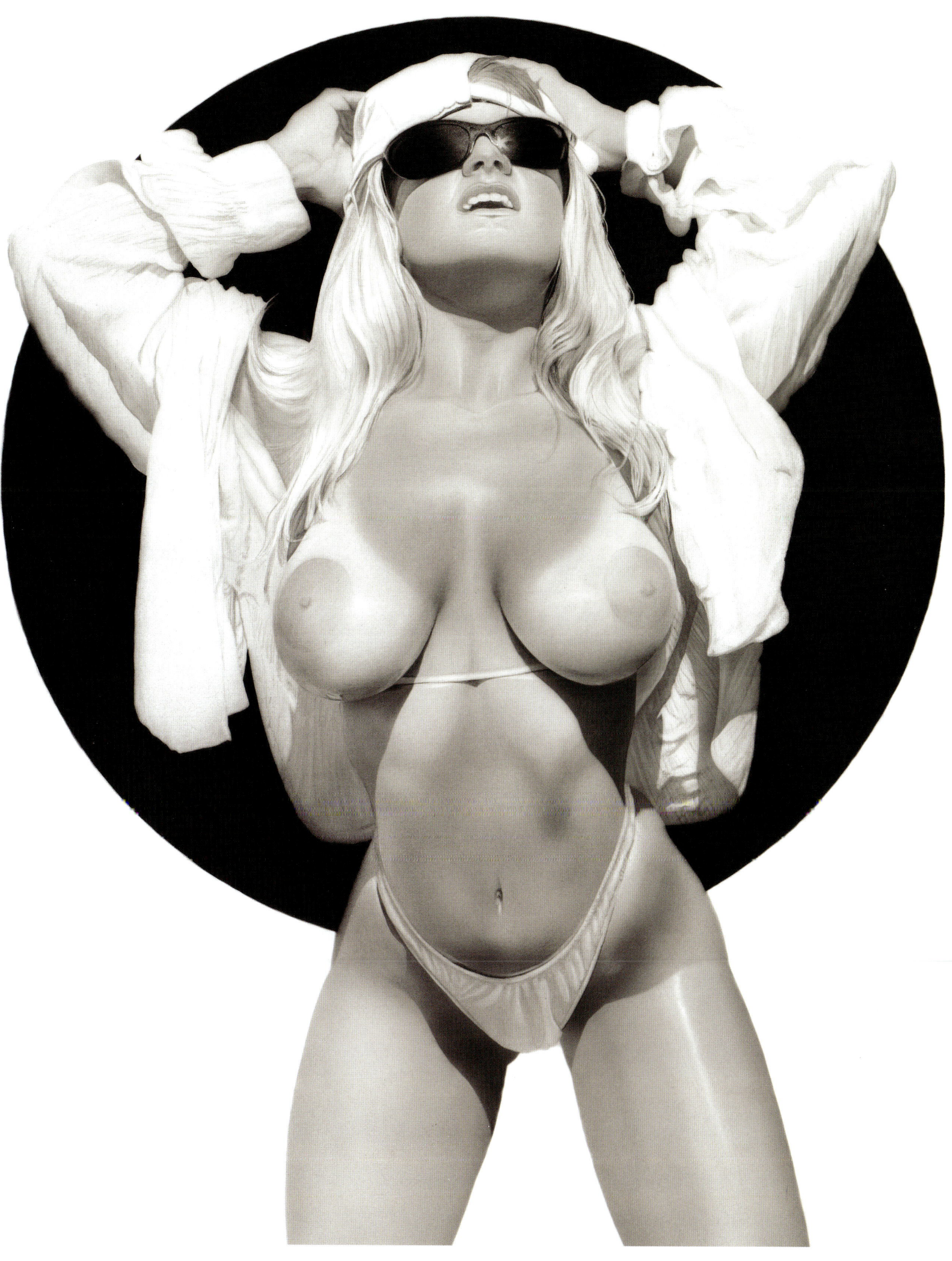

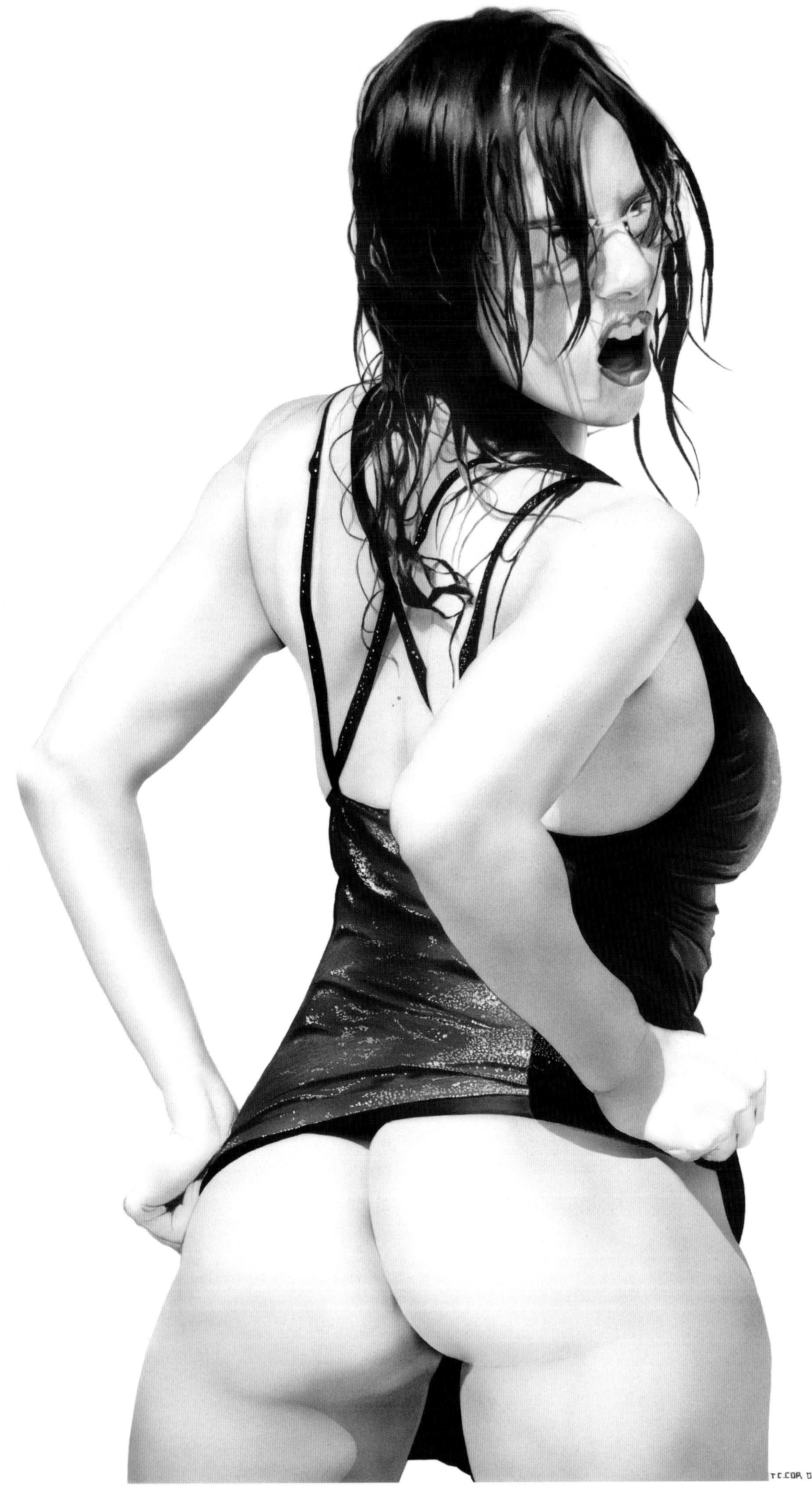
T.C.COR 06

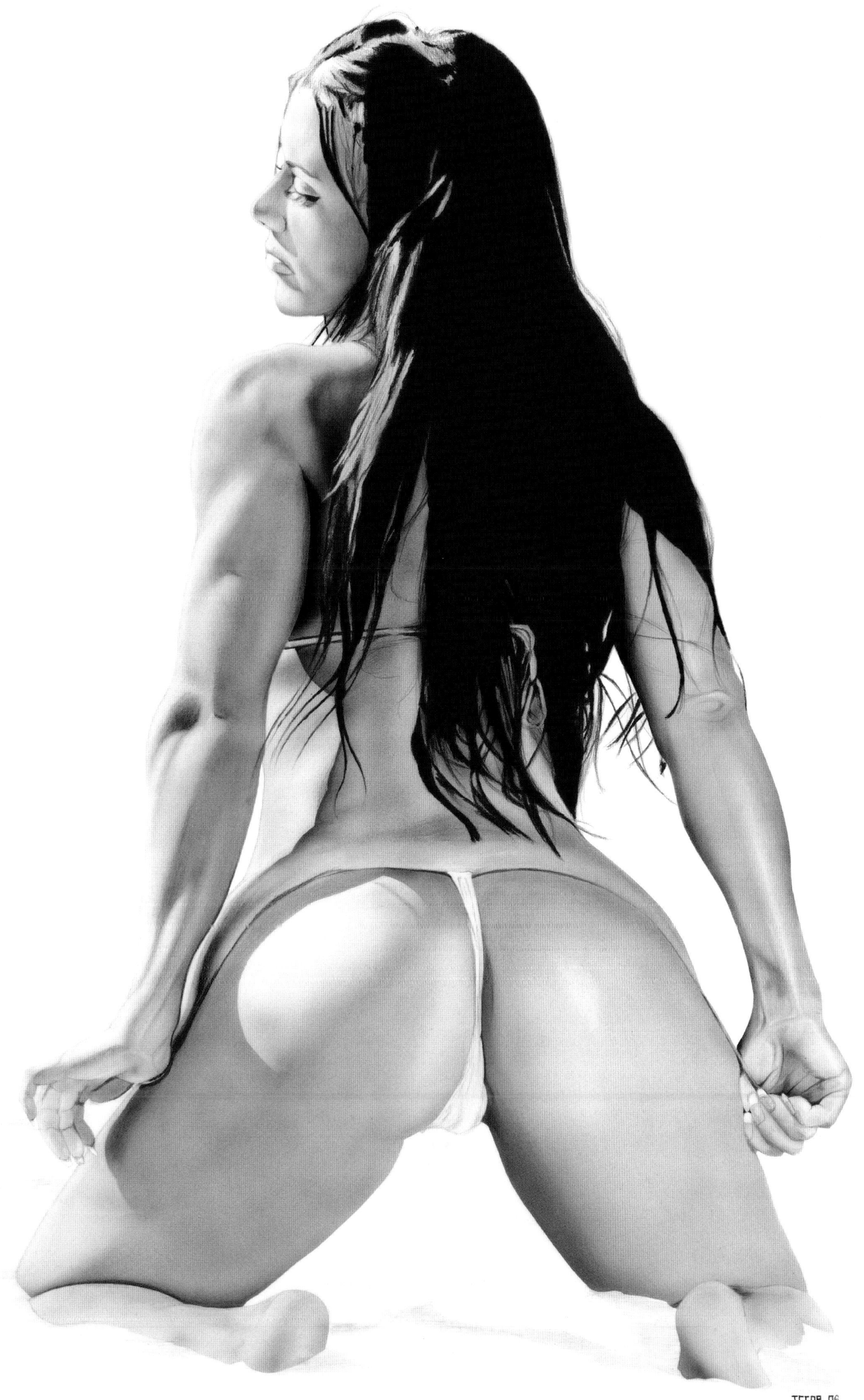
TCCOR 06

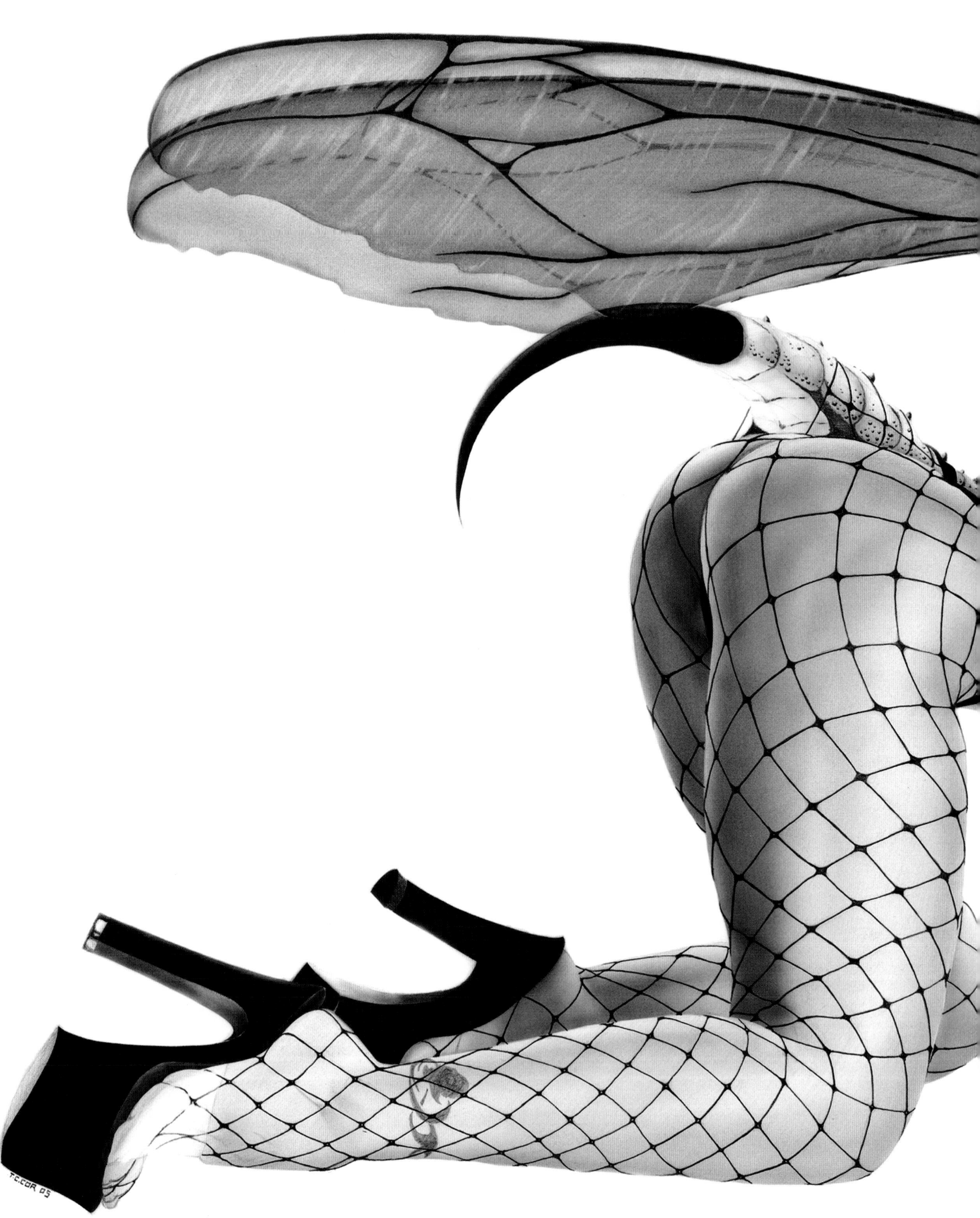
T.C.COR 05

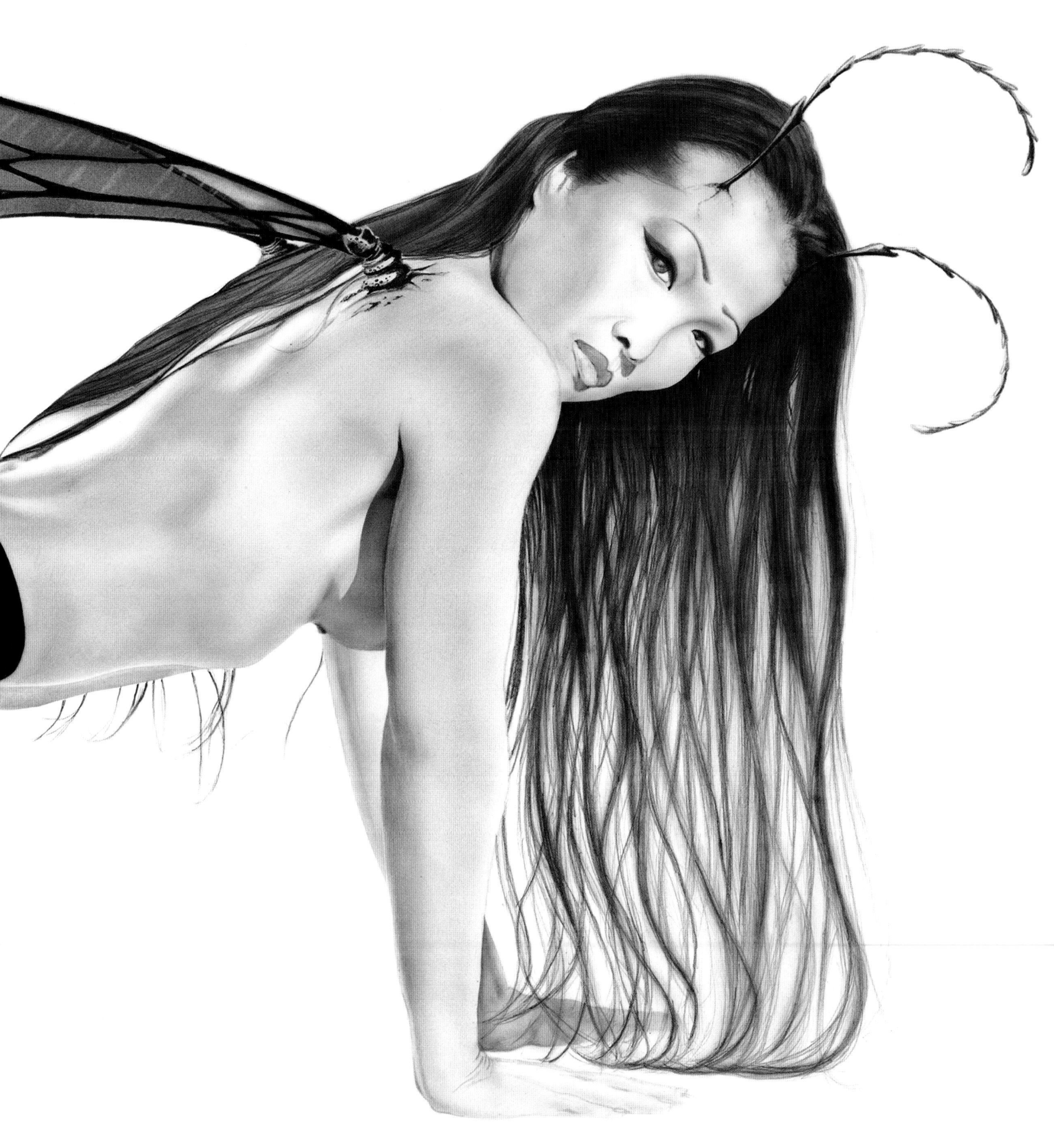

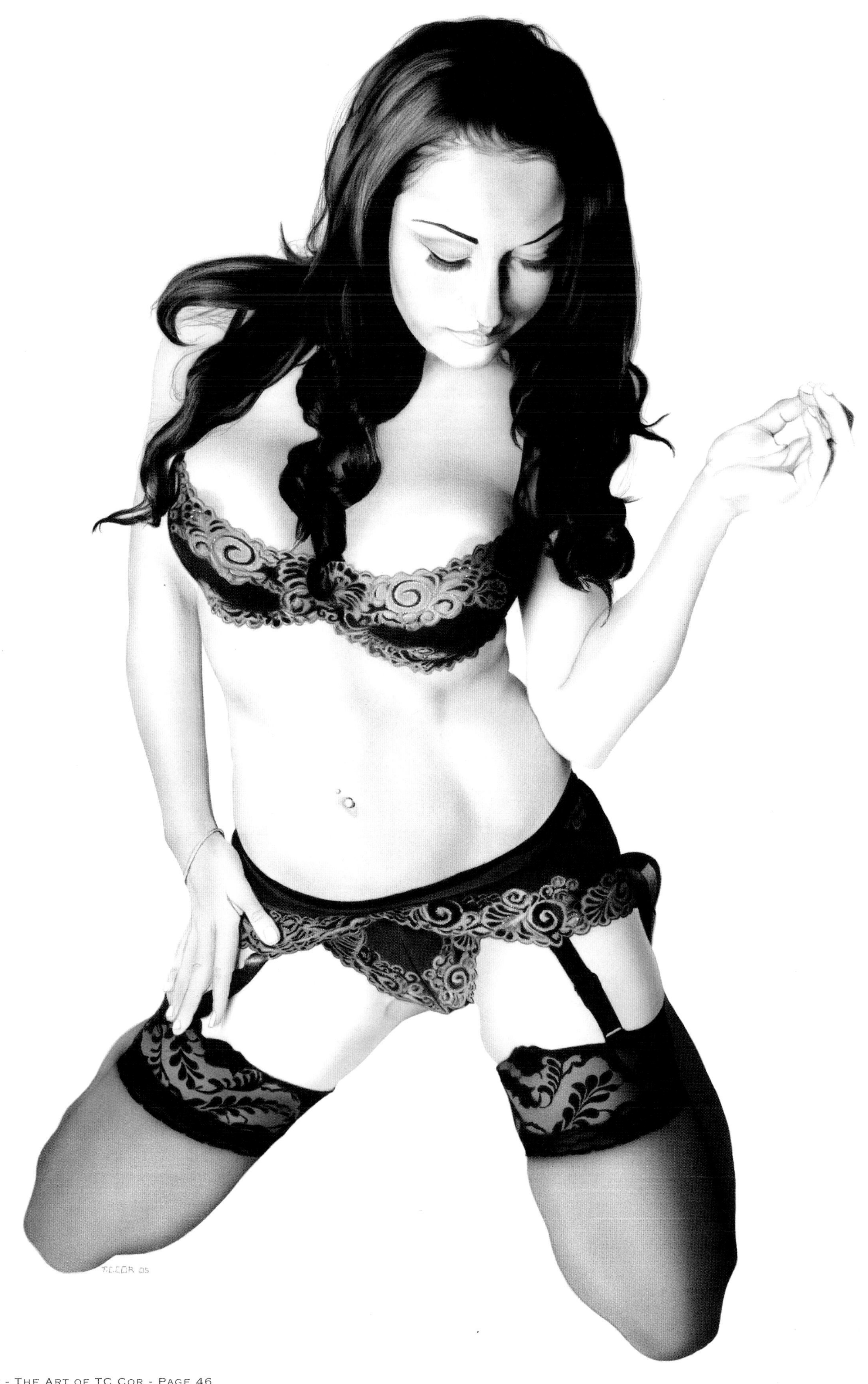

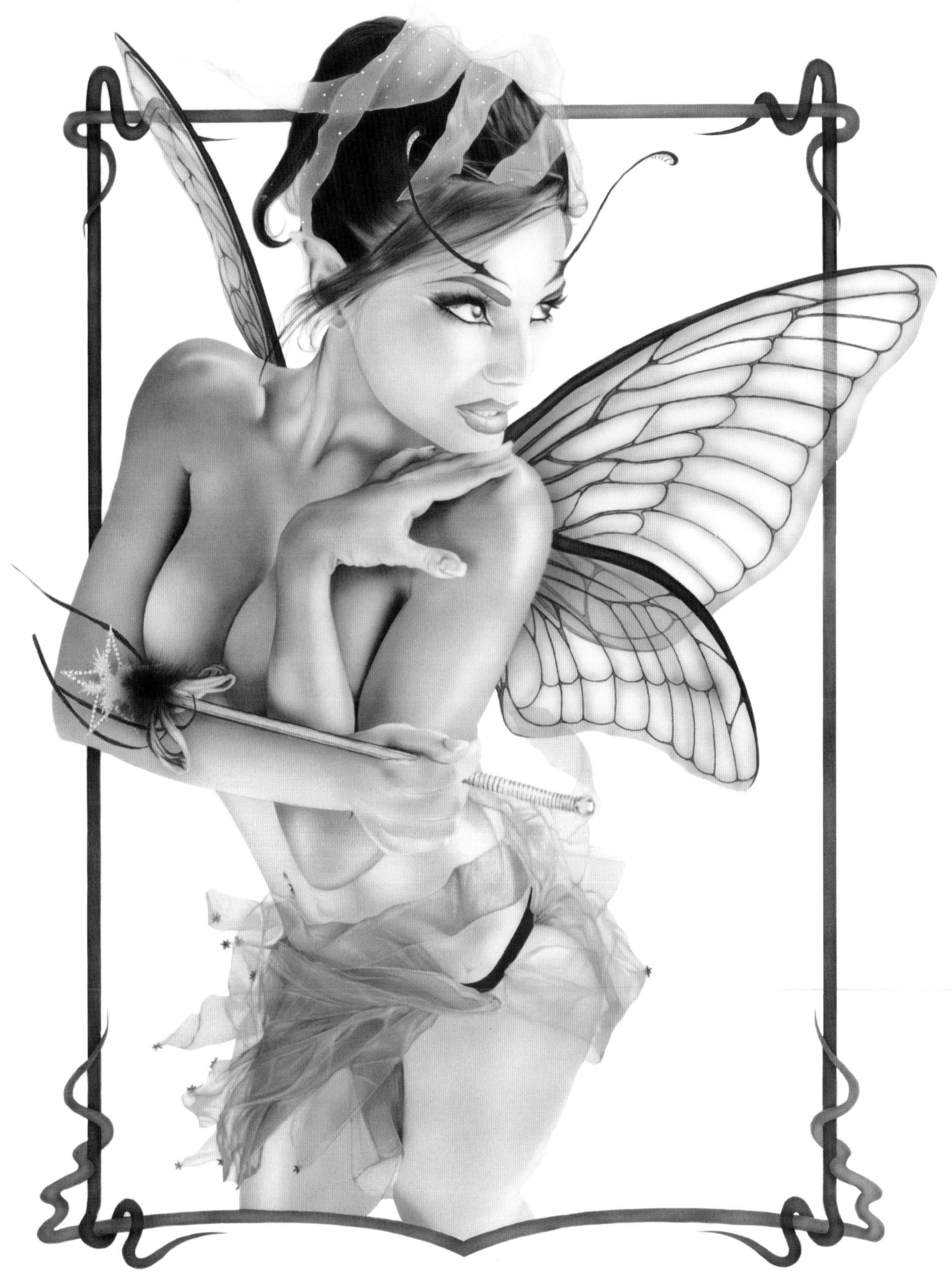

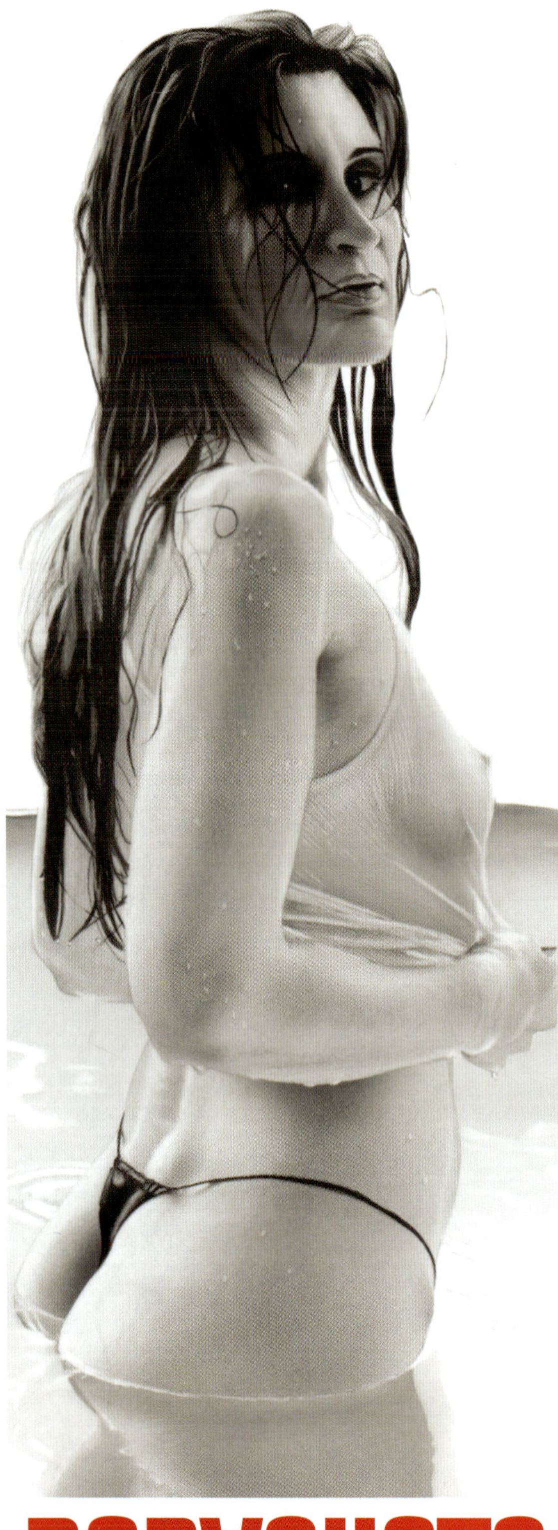

BODYSHOTS INDEX

Page 2 Butterfly - Model Karen Leigh Auger
Page 3 Alex 2 - Model Alex Del Monacco www.alexsplayground.com
Page 4 Chained - Model Megan Daniels www.megandanielsxo.com
Photo reference by Mike Prado Photography
Page 5 Are You Tipping - Photo reference by -Trev- wwwmodelmayhem.com/25292
Page 6-7 Aria 1-2 - Model: Aria Giovanni www.ariagiovanni.com
Photo reference by Arturo Jaurequi
Page 8 Drakaina - Model Drakaina www.drakaina.com
Page 9 Asian Rain - Model Vanna Marie www.modelmayhem.com/vannamarie
Photo reference by Moses G Marquez www.wepaymodels.com
Page 10-11 Curvylishous - Model Ifhegemeia www.modelmayhem.com/467946
Photo reference by Paul Reinquin www.paulreinquin.com
Page 12 Alex 1 - Model Alex Del Monacco www.alexsplayground.com
Page 13 Bound - Model Janine-May
Photo reference by David Leslie www.david-leslie.20mn.com
Page 14 Checkers - Model Amber Cristine www.modelmayhem.com/14633
Photo reference by Atomic Effect www.atomiceffect.com
Page 15 Clone - Model Jeannie Kayla www.modelmayhem.com/1070662
Photo reference by Manfred Keilnhofer www.keilnhofer.at/press/
Page 16 Down On You - Model Sabrina Fox www.facebook.com/thesabrinafox
Photo reference by Fox www.foxmanfotography.com
Page 17 Cowboy - Model Natalie Lynn www.modelmayhem.com/NatalieLynn
Photo reference by Kalen Foto www.modelmayhem.com/kalenphoto
Page 18 Drakaina - Model Drakaina www.drakaina.com
Page 19 Dressing Room - Photo reference by Brian D Perkins
www.modelmayhem.com/48563
Page 20-21 Desiree - Model Desiree Starr www.desireestarr.com
Photo reference by The Dark Slide
Page 22 Jayne - Photo reference by Victor Romero
Page 23 Leather - Model Jeska Vardinski www.jeskhotbox.com
Photo reference by RC Photo www.modelmayhem.com/rcphoto
Page 24 Lilly - Model Lilly Ruiz
Page 25 Morning Passion - Photo reference by Chris Thomson www.christhomson.com
Page 26 Pleasures Corner - Model Valya www.modelmayhem.com/ValyaSmetrova
Photo reference by Aldo Antonio
www.facebook.com/Aldo-Antonio-Photography
Page 27 Net - Model Kellie Maines www.modelmayhem.com/162574
Photo reference by AMaginations www.amaginations.com
Page 28-29 Lickem - Model Larisa Burdeynaya www.modelmayhem.com/6662
Photo reference by Elizabeth Zusev www.zusevdesigns.net/main/
Page 30-31 Overeasy 1-2 - Model Jossie www.facebook.com/jossie.ricanbombshell
Import Eye Candy studios www.iecstudios.com
Page 32 Pink Sheet - Commission piece model N/A
Page 33 Relax - Model Angela Ryan www.angelaryan.moonfruit.com
Photo reference by Christine Kessler www.modelmayhem.com/3924
Page 34 Red Corset - Model Shawna
Photo reference by Tim Heffernan Eros Studios
www.erosstudios.zenfolio.com
Page 35 Sivan - Model Sivan Krispin www.pinkiniswimwear.com
Photo reference by Jefferson Peak www.jeffersonpeak.com
Page 36-37 Trailer Darling - Model Trailer Darling www.modelmayhem.com/shanin
Photo reference by Jeff Fiore www.fiorephoto.tumblr.com
Page 38 Sophia - Model Sophia Innsbruck
Page 39 Serpent - Model Karol Helms www.modelmayhem.com/KarolHelms
Photo reference by NC Glamour www.modelmayhem.com/ncglamour
Page 40 Tearing Away - Model (Modelo) Tony A. Franklin
www.modelmayhem.com/Modelo
Page 41 Tanlines - Commission piece model N/A
Page 42 Pool Side - Model Nicole Ferreira www.nicoleferreira.com
Page 43 Beached - Tamar LiCalzi www.facebook.com/asktamar
Photo reference by Del Anthony www.modelmayhem.com/26698
Page 44-45 Wasp - Model Rayne Ahn www.modelmayhem.com/rayneahn
Page 46 Larisa - Model Larisa Burdeynaya www.modelmayhem.com/6662
Page 47 Glam Fairy - Model Claudia G. www.claudiag.net
Page 48 Model Karen Leigh Auger